"Authentic, evocative, and transformative, this journey of healing and hope captures the heart of any reader who has been a parent, a counselor, a peace officer or any combination of these."

—**Eve Myer**, Executive Director, San Francisco Suicide Prevention

"A riveting story of God's grace and healing in the face of the most profound loss and grief. Brian Cahill's compassionate work with both prisoners and law-enforcement officers, after the suicide of his son, is a compelling testimony of faith, hope and love."

—**James Martin**, Author of *Jesus a Pilgrimage*

"An inviting, palpable, powerhouse of a book, Cops, Cons and Grace takes us on a story we will never forget. From a father's deep, unconditional love of his son, John Francis Cahill, to the darkest depths of pain and despair after he loses his police officer son. This book will show you desperate hurt from such a loss, but more important, it brings us closer to the minds of officers to whom Brian gives the gift of hope every day. Brian Cahill is my new hero. This book will widen your lens, while opening your heart to healing, recovery, growth and grace from the abyss that is suicide."

—**Kevin Hines**, Author of *Cracked Not Broken, Surviving and Thriving After a Suicide Attempt*

"*Cops, Cons and Grace* is about two very different cultures and how these cultures offered peace and resolution after a suicide. It is a moving story about how the police and prison inmate cultures lead one man to forgive himself for his child's suicide. Ultimately the book is about the love a parent has for a child and what happens when that child commits suicide. It is moving, uplifting and informative. I highly recommend this book for anyone interested in the psychology of suicide survivors, anyone struggling with a suicide or someone simply interested in a moving story about love and forgiveness."

—**Joel Fay**, Co-author of *Counseling Cops, What Clinicians Need To Know*

"Brian Cahill found healing and strength in an unexpected place—with convicts at San Quentin state prison—after the suicide of his son, a 42-year-old police officer, plunged him into unimaginable grief. This gripping, personal and inspiring journey reveals the power of grace over death as the author channels his heartbreak into loving action, honoring his son's life by teaching suicide awareness and prevention to police officers. This is a timely and important book given the high risk of suicide among law-enforcement and correctional officers today, but will appeal to anyone who has wondered how to find hope amidst despair."

—**George Williams**, Catholic Chaplain, San Quentin State Prison

"Brian Cahill shares with the reader his experience living through the tragic loss of his firstborn son John, a police officer as a victim of police suicide. As a police psychologist, I personally found Mr. Cahill's work particularly on point to assist the law enforcement profession by bringing light to the tragic loss of life of fine young men and women who risk their life not only to violent crime, but to broken spirits. Psychologists, chaplains and administrators who work in the area of helping first responders need to read this book."

—**Kevin M Gilmartin**, Author of *Emotional Support for Law Enforcement*

"*Cops, Cons and Grace* is a wise and beautiful book about sorrow, grace and redemption. It will offer comfort to anyone who's grieving, hope to anyone in a dark place on their journey, and insight and instruction to anyone working in the area of suicide prevention with police officers."

—**Mary Allen**, Author of *Rooms of Heaven*

"Brian Cahill shares his journey before and after his son's suicide. It is an emotional roller coaster which probes into how his son, a police officer, tried to deal with stress and depression. As a retired cop who lost a colleague to suicide, this is an extremely important read."

—**Anthony Ribera**, Director, International Institute of Criminal Justice Leadership, University of San Francisco

"Brian Cahill has written a very personal story full of raw emotion and intense depth. Following the suicide of his police officer son, Cahill embarks on a passionate journey looking for reassurance of God's presence and trying to make sense of life and death. Written by (in Cahill's own words) 'a father who's immobilized by horror and pain', he nonetheless finds comfort, support and answers in some usual, and unusual places. Anyone who has lost a loved one to suicide will be helped by this story. This is a book full of grace."

—**Ron Rolheiser**, Author, Columnist and President of Oblate School of Theology

Cops, Cons, and Grace

Cops, Cons, and Grace

A Father's Journey Through His Son's Suicide

Brian Cahill

Foreword by Dan Willis

RESOURCE *Publications* · Eugene, Oregon

Cops, Cons, and Grace
A Father's Journey Through His Son's Suicide

Resource Publications
An Imprint of Wipf and Stock Publishers
199 W. 8th Ave., Suite 3
Eugene, OR 97401

www.wipfandstock.com

PAPERBACK ISBN: 978-1-5326-3500-7
HARDCOVER ISBN: 978-1-5326-3502-1
EBOOK ISBN: 978-1-5326-3501-4

Manufactured in the U.S.A.

To Donna, who keeps me breathing
and to Kristine and Kaitlin

He who learns must suffer. And even in our sleep, pain, which cannot forget, falls drop by drop upon the heart, until in our own despair, against our will, comes wisdom through the awful grace of God.

—AESCHYLUS

From the beginning, cops are taught to maintain an occupational persona: a "public face" that makes them always appear to be in control, on top of things, knowledgeable and unafraid.

—ELLEN KIRSCHMAN, *I LOVE A COP*

One thing I know for sure: Death is not the end of the story.

—MARY ALLEN, *THE ROOMS OF HEAVEN*

Contents

Foreword

I HAVE BEEN INSPIRED by the compassion, wisdom, and especially the depth of love Brian Cahill has displayed since the first time I spoke with him. In the summer of 2015 Brian called me after a professional editor I had previously worked with gave him my contact information. I am a retired police captain whose first book, an emotional survival and wellness guidebook for first responders called *Bulletproof Spirit: The First Responder's Essential Resource for Protecting and Healing Mind and Heart*, had recently been released.

That summer afternoon I found myself speaking with the grieving father of a 19-year veteran police officer who had killed himself in December, 2008. Brian, determined to honor his beloved son and wanting to save other officers from taking their own lives, had courageously written this powerful account of John's life and death that will bring comfort, hope, a path toward healing, and peace to persons suffering from loss or trauma.

One year later, on July 11, 2016, I sat across a San Francisco restaurant table from Brian and his most gracious wife, Donna. Brian, who has been telling his son's story and speaking of suicide awareness and prevention every week for the past several years to the San Francisco Police Department, had helped to arrange for me to present emotional survival tips to some of their officers. As you read these pages depicting a father's love, you will be deeply moved by the depth of beauty of this man's heart— just as I was that evening.

Brian's tale of the tragic loss of his dear son is a remarkable journey of the soul—from despair to hope; grieving to purpose; insufferable pain to the healing balm of grace. This painful journey of healing reveals the inherent spirituality within all life and the greatest need for us all: to give love, to be loved, to express love—and to help others.

What is God's grace, but divine love, healing and inspiring our heart and comforting our soul? Brian's tragic loss and suffering would have suffocated his heart, were it not for his love for his son, the love of his dear wife, and his devotion to serve and help others—allowing his grieving heart a new outlet to express the deep love within himself. Remarkably, Brian even finds great comfort, wisdom, love, and support from prison inmates, some convicted of murder, through the spiritual group he co-leads each week within the walls of San Quentin prison. Love's influence comes from all sources, even the most unlikely; grace to breathe life back into our heart is all around us.

Brian's profound experiences of loss, suffering, healing, and forgiveness make clear that love never dies; it is never diminished, as it is as eternal as God. He shares that there is never any separateness—even though our loved ones may precede us in our return Home in God. Love is the abiding grace that not only connects, but heals, blesses, and comforts. While one's heart is suffocating, the mystery of grace is at work to restore peace. The mystery of grace is the eternal power within the healing infinitudes of love; Brian shares that gratitude is the open door to experience this graciousness of God.

This is not a book just for those grieving the loss of a loved one, but for every police officer and first responder as well. Trauma injures and poisons the soul. Whether trauma is experienced through great loss and suffering, or through the myriad experiences of a police officer, trauma can kill. It can slowly disintegrate the spirit of life within; it can suffocate your heart. Yet Brian's message is that there is grace within suffering—there is life after trauma, tragedy, and loss. It comes through finding new outlets to express love, service, and compassion—not to replace the love of a lost loved one, but to honor it, expand it, and share it with others.

Brian is perhaps more uniquely qualified to write this book than most. A man who devoted his professional life of 40 years to compassionate social service, with his last ten years before retirement as the head of San Francisco Catholic Charities; a devoted and loving father of a 19-year police veteran; a spiritual group leader to San Quentin lifers who have found grace's healing potential through their own tragedies—Brian combines these unique experiences into a hopeful message of healing and peace for everyone. Forgive, especially yourself; find ways to express your love; honor those departed by choosing to live a more purposeful life; cultivate a consciousness of gratitude; help and serve others.

As a former police officer who served for nearly 30 years, I know the effects of trauma. Suicide is the #1 cause of death every year for officers, with another nearly one in five suffering from post-traumatic stress. Every police officer and first responder is vulnerable to the trauma of their profession, which can easily and all too often does spiral into suicidal ideation. The nearly 150 officers who killed themselves last year—all thought it would never happen to them. Officers' natural abilities to be resilient and to cope lessen over time as a result of their career experiences; they tend to lose perspective, become despondent, depressed, and at times feel lost and hope-less with their lives seemingly out of control. This book shows that there are paths toward healing, restoration, and peace. It describes the devastation left behind any suicide. No family member is ever better off because some-one chooses to take their own life. I know firsthand the healing, peace, and comfort that is offered through Brian's eloquent message.

Brian writes, "I began to write this book to try to lessen my own pain. I hope that my writing might possibly lessen the pain for others and provide them some small portion of comfort." You will find, as I did, that Brian's words of grace are far more than comforting; they will speak to your heart. They offer healing, insight, inspiration, and peace.

Dan Willis, San Marcos, CA
Captain (ret.) La Mesa Police
Founder, FirstResponderWellness.com
Author, *Bulletproof Spirit*

Preface

I STARTED WRITING THIS book as a way to honor my son, John Francis Cahill. That is still my goal. But I've learned that this kind of writing carries the writer through multiple stages of awareness and discovery.

Early on I realized I wanted my writing to provide comfort for my granddaughters, to help them really know their father, to help them survive their father's suicide, and to help them live lives that would make their dad a symbol of hope and life rather than despair and death.

I was not far into the writing when I became aware that I belonged to a group of special human beings. The literature calls us suicide survivors, but we are parents, grandparents, spouses, partners, siblings, and children of a loved one who lost their way. And now, because I know the pain of my fellow survivors, and because I began to write this book to try to lessen my own pain, I hope that my story might possibly lessen the pain for others and provide them some small portion of comfort.

As I learned about cops and suicide, I came to hope that my writing would help police officers and their families have a better understanding of the hidden risks of police work and perhaps be instrumental in reducing the number of law enforcement suicides. That has become my major goal in writing this book. This is the most concrete way I can think to honor my son and help cops, especially at a time when police officers are under more pressure and stress than at any other time in the history of law enforcement.

When I was far along in the depths of writing this book, I also began to see that my writing was exploring the relationship between grief and grace, pain and grace. This is a theme addressed by many writers, but I personally had never before made the connection between pain and grace, let alone thought I would write about it. As a Catholic, I was familiar with the concept that the cross is followed by the resurrection, and that from death comes new life. But for me it was only a concept. Sometime after John died I began to experience it in a real way; I began to sense that new life truly does come after death, that John was somehow still with us. I also, very slowly, experienced my own resurrection after John's death. And as I was writing about John's suicide and my life afterward, I began to glimpse this mysterious, symbiotic connection between pain and grace. I began to feel it in my bones. And I began to experience grace in unexpected places, including the suicide prevention training I do with cops, and, even more unexpectedly, in San Quentin prison, where I lead a weekly spirituality group for fifteen lifers. I hope that my reflections can be of some comfort to those, whether they're religious or not, who have lost a loved one to suicide. And I hope that for them grief can lead to grace.

Acknowledgements

To Mary Allen, author of *The Rooms of Heaven*. There is no book without Mary—my instructor at the Iowa Summer Writing Festival, my writing coach, my editor, my mentor, and my friend. To Julie McCarron for editing my book proposal and final manuscript, and for her friendship, support and perseverance with me in trying to get this book out. To the team at Wipf and Stock, for taking a chance on me, and especially to James Stock, Matt Wimer, Brian Palmer, RaeAnne Harris, and Daniel Lanning.

To my counselor Janet Childs at the Center for Living with Dying in San Jose, who kept me together, and to my spiritual director Bernie Bush, SJ, who kept my soul together. To Dr. Adina Shore who kept our family together, and to Patrick Arbore who directs the Grief Support Group at the San Francisco Institute on Aging—for his wisdom and compassion, and for making me realize I wanted to write about John; and to my fellow grief support group members for their wisdom and support.

To Michael Leach, Kevin Hines, Michael Krasny, Richard Lischer, Joan Wickersham, Claire Gerus, Roger Freet, John Gehring, Sarah Stanton, Kitty Moore, Cynthia Sigmund, John Brooks, Judy Nelson, Mike Marovich and Lanny Vincent for their support along the way.

To James Martin, SJ, whose writing has comforted me and whose support has motivated me. To Father Ron Rolheiser for his early encouragement and for his syndicated columns on suicide, a source of comfort for me and for many others.

To John Diaz and Lois Kasakoff at the *San Francisco Chronicle*, Tom Fox and Dennis Coday at the *National Catholic Reporter*, and Barbara Keenlyside when she was at CNN Online, all of whom gave me a chance to write about cops and suicide.

To Amy Margolis and the folks at the Iowa Summer Writing Festival who create a safe and welcoming environment for those of us who want to write but start off not knowing what we're doing.

To retired San Francisco Police Chief Tony Ribera for encouraging me to start speaking about cops and suicide. To retired Sgt. Mary Dunnigan,

Sgt. Art Howard, and the team at the SFPD Behavioral Science Unit for the unsung work they do supporting cops, and for their compassion and support as I joined them. To Sgt. Vanessa Payne of the San Jose PD Crisis Management Unit and her predecessor, Sgt. Teresa Jeglum, for their support and friendship. To Joel Fay of the First Responders Support Network and the team at FRSN, and to Kevin Gilmartin and Dan Willis for their great writing and work in providing emotional support for cops and all first responders. And to Andy O'Hara, Ron Clark, and John Violanti at The Badge of Life for helping reduce the number of cops who lose their way. To Ellen Kirschman for her great writing about what cops and their families need, and for her never-ending support in helping me get this book published. I have learned from all of these professionals and this is a better book because of them.

To San Quentin Chaplain George Williams, SJ, former chaplain Steven Barber, SJ, and my brothers at San Quentin, some of who are free today, all of who unknowingly helped me write this book. I've changed their names, but their stories are real and their impact on me is real.

To Rita Semel who told me I had a choice: to retreat from life or find a way to honor John. And to Maureen, Rachel, Mary, Gloria and Moe, Erica and John, Olga and Miguel—all of whom lost a child this way—they reminded me I was not alone.

To my dear friends Joe and Dianne Harrington and John and Phyllis Van Hagen, for their love and friendship and for their willingness to let me blabber endlessly about the book.

My love, respect and gratitude to my son Ed, professor of English at Fordham, who told me to write my truth, and to Ed's partner, the writer Mark Jude Poirier, who pointed me to Iowa and to Mary Allen. To my daughter Danielle for her love and support.

And finally to Donna Cahill, who not only keeps me breathing but also served as my final reader of this book, as she is the final reader for almost all other major aspects of my life. I love you, Donna Maria.

Prologue

August 2005

On a rare sunny day in summertime San Francisco, my wife Donna and I putter around the house preparing for a small family dinner. Late in the afternoon, when we hear my son John's car pull up outside, we open our front door and smilingly await the onslaught. Kaitlin, our energetic seven-year-old granddaughter, pops out of the car, races up the steps and leaps into my arms. "Hi Grandpa!" Before I know it, she's wriggled out of my arms and jumped into Donna's warm embrace.

John, laughing, follows his daughter up the stairs. He is a tanned, solidly built six-footer whose cropped brown hair is just starting to recede. He has warm brown eyes and a thick brown mustache. My firstborn, police officer, father of my granddaughters—my beautiful boy, my rock. We hug each other. We don't say anything. We don't have to.

John gives Donna a hug and strokes her hair fondly—a signature gesture he reserves for his favorite people. As I look at my son with my wife I realize how genuinely close they have become. This bond comes from John's appreciation that my second wife has truly given me a second chance at life and happiness. For her part, Donna knew from the start how close my son and I have always been. She took him immediately and unreservedly into her heart along with his two daughters.

Kaitlin is her usual lively, bubbly self. Observing her and seeing nothing amiss gives me some immediate relief from my lingering worry. There has been tension in her parents' relationship for some time now, and Donna and I have been concerned about its impact on our little one.

While Kaitlin helps Grandma Donna prepare dinner, John and I grab a couple of Heinekens and head out to the deck overlooking Donna's backyard vegetable garden. We sit quietly for a while, enjoying the last of the sun's warmth as it slowly moves beyond the back of our house. As we savor our sharp, icy beers, we are both comfortable with the silence. The two of us have always been easy together without feeling the need to talk, whether it's on a backpacking trail, working a trout stream, or just sitting on a deck.

Finally, I ask, "How are things on the home front?" John sighs. "Some big ups, some big downs, but it's all going to work out. I think Michele wants this marriage to work. I know I do." I know enough about the situation to be a bit concerned that things may not be fixable. I hesitate, not wanting to offer unwanted advice, but finding it hard to keep silent as I remember my own divorce from John's mother.

Still, John looks good, appears relaxed and optimistic. Surely this is just one of the bumps in the road of any long marriage. "Dad, you don't have to worry," he says affectionately, catching my mood and seeing that I am holding myself back. "Like I said, it's all going to work out. Now, how about another Heineken?"

After I return with two more beers I move to safer and happier ground. I ask John how work is going. John has been a cop for sixteen years. He loves the work and is very good at it. He tells me about arresting some bad guys who had been attacking women in a supermarket parking lot. He takes a swig of his beer, sets it firmly on the table with an audible thump and concludes, "I hope they're locked up for a long time."

Given John's last comment, I realize that I have to tell my son about my volunteer work at San Quentin, something I haven't quite gotten around to discussing with him even though we speak all the time. The truth is that, without even being consciously aware of it, I've been putting this discussion off. So I tell him what I've been doing one night a week for the past few months. It started in the spring, when, as the head of San Francisco Catholic Charities, I was asked by a group of Catholic inmates at San Quentin to help them write a paper on restorative justice.

The goal of restorative justice is to help offenders gain insight and remorse for their actions, enabling them to take responsibility for their crimes through focusing on the needs and perspectives of victims and their families. I helped the men write the part of the paper dealing with the social services needs of both the victims' and inmates' families. The inmates planned to present the paper to California's Catholic bishops in the hope that the bishops would use the information to influence public policy.

Over the course of many meetings with the inmates as we drafted the paper, I came to see beyond the stereotype of "convict" and "murderer." I began to see each inmate as an individual, each in his own way on a journey of faith. I came to know many of the men personally, to learn about their offenses, their family situations, their hopes for release, and their faith.

There is so much I want to say to John about what I've learned about the system. Most of the men I know were sentenced to fifteen years to life for second-degree murder—almost invariably drug or alcohol-related—at a very young age. According to the law, inmates who meet all the criteria for rehabilitation and have no behavior problems are eligible for parole within twelve to eighteen years. But because no governor wants to be perceived as soft on crime or take a chance on a parolee reoffending, most of these men have been denied parole repeatedly and are serving time far beyond their original sentences.

But John is a cop, well aware of the law and sworn to uphold it. He is unlikely to be moved by their situation, so I focus on what I think will reach him. I tell him that the recidivism rate for fixed-term parolees is 70 percent, but the recidivism rate for this particular group—rehabilitated "lifers" who do manage to finally get out—is under 2 percent. I stress that I remind myself on a regular basis that the men I've come to know are not necessarily representative of the larger prison population.

When I stop speaking John doesn't respond. I turn to him in the fading light. "What are you thinking?" He looks away and says, "Dad, I don't know—these guys have done really bad things. They deserve to be exactly where they are." I look at my son the cop, respecting who he is and the difficult job he does, but wanting him—perhaps needing him—to approve of what I feel increasingly called to do.

I launch into a passionate commentary about the men I'm working with, explaining that these are real people I have come to know, not statistics. I talk about the education they have received, their insight, remorse, and hard-won maturity. I become indignant as I talk about their long journey, their struggle to hold on to hope and faith after serving decades beyond their original sentences. Now John is watching me closely. I see he's taking it all in, but there's skepticism on his face, a look that tells me that he's still not buying what I'm selling.

I stand up and lean my back against the railing of the deck. "So let me ask you something," I challenge him. "When you're out on patrol next Monday night, which guy do you want to have to deal with, one of my guys, whose recidivism rate is next to nothing, or some young, violent knucklehead? Some kid who's just hitting the streets after five years locked up, someone who regrets nothing and hasn't learned one damn thing?"

John puts down his beer, throws up his hands in mock surrender and says, "Okay, okay! You've convinced me." By now he's smiling. He stands up, picks up his beer, raises it and says, "To my Dad, a great social worker." I raise my beer in return. "To my son, a great cop."

I'm relieved but not surprised that John has given me his blessing for my work at San Quentin. I am so proud of him. My concern about the state of his marriage is outweighed by my confidence in his ability to make everything right. I put my arm around him and we head inside, toward the light and the delicious smells and the sound of Donna and Kaitlin laughing. I'm blessed to have such a strong, healthy, secure, and loving man as my firstborn. A good cop, a great father, a wonderful son. He's my rock. He will always be my rock.

1

He's My Rock

IT IS ALMOST THREE years later, in the spring of 2008, when John and I meet again for dinner—this time just the two of us. I have spent the day in Scotts Valley, an hour south of San Francisco, the suburb where John makes his home. Earlier we watched Kaitlin play in a sixth-grade basketball game. After the game John returned to his new apartment. He's been separated from Michele and living in his own place for two months.

I drive over to his old house to hang out with Kaitlin for a while after the game. Michele greets me at the door with a gentle hug. Early in the divorce proceedings, Michele told us that she was afraid we would reject her. Donna and I assured her that while we supported John we did not intend to condemn anybody, especially the mother of our granddaughters. But standing there at the front door of the house where my son lived for so long, Michele and I are both aware of how much our relationship has changed. To avoid any further awkwardness, I suggest taking Kaitlin to the local ice cream store, and Michele readily—gratefully—agrees.

After I drop Kaitlin back at the house I head out to meet up with John at his favorite local Italian restaurant. I get there early and get seated. The waiter brings over two menus. I glance at mine and then look up as John walks through the door. He's wearing jeans, hiking boots, a faded olive polo shirt and his favorite tan suede jacket. I'm wearing jeans, hiking boots, and a fleece. It occurs to me that much of the time we spend together we wear jeans and hiking boots.

John sits down heavily in his seat across the table from me. He looks tired but determined. I remember that look from when he was just a kid and something went wrong. Sports or girls, 4-H or school—John always faced his problems head on. He would figure out how to solve the problem, remedy the error and get back in the game. He picks up the menu and studies the familiar selections carefully. Earlier, as we sat in the bleachers in the gym at Kaitlin's school, he'd told me how depressed he was about the divorce. "I'm depressed but that doesn't mean I'm not hungry," he says now. He looks up and gives me a small smile. I'm thankful he hasn't lost his sense of humor.

We order steaks and a bottle of Cabernet. As we eat he tells me that he's still hoping for a respectful, peaceful settlement, and doing all he can to ensure that Kaitlin and Krissy won't be permanently hurt by the divorce. Then—and these are the words I'll return to over and over again, in my mind, much later—that he's looking forward to moving through this painful time and coming out the other end.

I look him in the eye and tell him with complete certainty that I know he'll survive, and that just as I came through my own painful divorce from his mother, he too will emerge to find another relationship and a happier life. Just as I found Donna, he will find someone new to love. I believe this because of his strength and determination, because of his love for his daughters and his love of life—and because of my still-rampant optimism, my yet-to-be-penetrated confidence, my utter obliviousness to how fragile life truly is. There is no doubt in my mind that my son will soon emerge, a stronger and wiser man, at the other end of this ordeal.

* * *

Eight months later the days are gray and gloomy, and it's dark by the time John parks his new gray Honda truck in front of our house late on Saturday afternoon of the long Thanksgiving weekend. There's also someone new in the passenger seat. Alisa, the young woman John has been seeing, greets us warmly. Alisa is an emergency room nurse. She and John started dating recently, which I thought was a good sign. Soon she retreats with Donna and Kaitlin to the kitchen, where their laughter and chatter floats outside on the chilly air. John and I and take our usual places on the deck. I study him closely as I hand him a beer.

John's in his usual off-duty attire: jeans, hiking boots and a flannel shirt. He looks tired, and the familiar sadness in his eyes worries me. His face is thinner, and it's clear he's lost weight in the past few weeks. I ask him how he's doing. He looks at me and says, "I'm down but I'm maintaining." My heart aches for my son and what he's going through. What can I do to help him? The years play back in a series of snapshots in my head. How have matters come to this?

* * *

John and Michele married in 1993. Krissy, Michele's daughter from her first marriage, was only four years old when my son entered her life. John, wanting to do everything right, took a course in step-parenting. He quickly came to love Krissy as his own, as did I. Michele took a picture of Krissy with John during the courtship. In the photo the tiny girl is seated on John's powerful motorcycle while John stands next to her wearing his uniform, watching her carefully. The look on both their faces shows how closely they have bonded.

When they married, John became an instant stepfather and I became an instant grandfather. When Krissy was in her teens and old enough to make and carry out the decision, she officially changed her last name to Cahill. Meanwhile, Kaitlin came along to complete the family. Their future looked so bright.

Thirteen years later, it has all come to ashes. I flash on the day John had haltingly told me that he had finally realized that his marriage was truly failing. He stopped and looked at me silently for a few moments, struggling to get out the words he hated having to say. Finally he told me he wasn't sure that Michele wanted to stay married. He said he had always thought he could make things right, but now he wasn't sure.

Years later, long after John was gone, I would read *The Suicide Index* by Joan Wickersham, a memoir about her father's suicide. She wrote about her dad: "He thought if he willed everything to be all right, then it would be. He thought if he could make it all look a certain way, solid and healthy, then it actually would be solid and healthy."

Like this father, as with John and maybe even with me, this wasn't hypocrisy or phoniness but rather a hope, a desire, a vision, a need for everything to be right and good. John tried to do in his marriage exactly what I had tried to do in my marriage to his mother. Neither of us succeeded.

As I run through the past couple of years in my mind, I can fix on the summer of 2007 as the time it became clear that John's marriage had irretrievably fallen apart. John was heartbroken and worried about the impact of divorce on Kaitlin. Because Krissy was working, going to school and living independently in her own apartment, John was less concerned about the immediate impact of the divorce on her, yet he sought to maintain a close relationship. When he and Michele officially decided to end their marriage, rather than retain opposing counsel, both agreed to legal mediation. They also jointly decided to put their house on the market.

John and I talked frequently that fall. He was worried about Kaitlin but trying to move through his pain and sadness and beginning to glimpse the possibility of a new life. I tried to reinforce the idea of a new life by continually reminding him that after my divorce I had been blessed with the opportunity for a new, loving relationship.

One night during that time, just after John and Michele had told Kaitlin that they were divorcing, Donna and I had dinner with our son and granddaughter at a restaurant in Scotts Valley. We knew that John was down and were impressed by how sensitive he was to Kaitlin's needs. Kaitlin, coloring on the placemat with crayons supplied by the waiter, didn't respond when he talked to her. John looked at her, stroked her hair, and said, "It's okay to be angry. This is hard and painful, and it's not fair to you, but don't ever think it is your fault, because it's not." Kaitlin looked at him, nodded, and continued to color. I loved that John was so responsive to her. Later I would make sure to caution him, "You also need to take care of yourself."

John and Kaitlin spent the first Christmas post-separation with us. When they arrived Kaitlin was excited to see us, and John appeared cheerful enough. Kaitlin stayed in the kitchen with Donna while John and I took a walk around the neighborhood. I told him he didn't have to hide his feelings from me. He looked at me but didn't say anything. In his eyes I saw how much pain he was in, the pain that comes from a mix of panic and shame and the realization that life has turned upside-down. I remembered those feelings well from the first Christmas after my own marriage ended.

A few days after Christmas, John's close friends and I helped him move into the new place near Kaitlin's school. As I carried furniture and boxes up the stairs to his condo, I remembered how, eleven years earlier, John had helped me move into my own apartment after my marriage to his mother broke up. While we were doing the moving, Donna took Kaitlin shopping for necessities and decorations for her new bedroom at her dad's. Grandma Donna—intuitive soul, child development professional—was watching Kaitlin like a hawk.

That night we ate at a nearby restaurant, and John reminded Kaitlin that his new place was right across the street from her school. He said that while living situations had changed he would see her during the week and part of every weekend, and that her parents and her grandparents all loved her very much. She looked at him for a long moment, almost as though she was questioning what he had just said. He put his arm around her, and finally she smiled, reassured.

* * *

By the spring of 2008 John and I had gotten into the habit of having long phone conversations every Thursday night, the beginning of his weekend. John was juggling work, spending time with his daughter, and handling divorce-related matters. Over time, he filled me in on specifics: the financial impact of the divorce, issues with putting the house on the market, his ongoing concern for Kaitlin's emotional wellbeing. He spoke of his own sadness. He realized he was grieving not only over his divorce, but the loss of his ideals and all he had once hoped his own marriage and family would be.

I told him that I understood what he was going through, and that just as he had been there for me during my divorce, I would be there for him now. I would be his rock. On March 30, on what would be his last birthday, Donna and I sent him a card telling him that things would get better "because of who you are, because of how you are handling this, and because God loves you and so do we."

John and Michele settled their finances in April, with the divorce to be finalized in June. John had surgery for a kidney stone but recovered rapidly. The house still wasn't selling. Kaitlin graduated from elementary school and seemed to be handling the changes in her life as well as could be expected. John, too, appeared to be slogging his way through this painful time as best he could. I announced my retirement from Catholic Charities, effective December.

That June John wrote in his Father's Day card to me, "Dad, you have been my rock this year. I love you so much." By July John was increasingly worried about the impact of the divorce on Kaitlin even though she seemed to be handling things well. Just to be safe he got her into counseling. He told me how frustrated he was about losing all the equity in the house, which still had not sold. At the end of August John started to see his own counselor, not just about his depression and sense of failure but also about his anger and frustration toward Michele. On my birthday card in September, John wrote again, "Dad, you have been my rock. I love you and I am so proud to be your son."

One day in October John drove up and we took a long walk at Fort Funston, above the beach in the southwest corner of San Francisco. As we walked with the wind from the ocean beating against us, John told me he'd had an anxiety attack. I'd seen my son sad and frustrated over the past year, but this marked the first time I heard panic in his voice and saw real fear in his eyes. As always, I tried to reassure him that this was a normal stage and these feelings, too, would pass. He looked at me and nodded. As the wind died down we stood together in silence on the bluff, looking out at the gray ocean and the blue and orange sky, watching the sun drop below the horizon. I hated that he was in so much pain, but I knew from my own experience—or I thought I knew—that John's pain would not last, that he would come through this, that he would survive.

Later we had dinner at a local Italian place, where we ordered pasta and Chianti. I raised my glass to John, "To my son. This will get better." He looked at me with sad eyes and said, "I don't know." He told me that for the first time in his life he was in a situation he felt completely unable to control and that he was frightened and depressed. He was also completely thrown because he'd been sure he was over the worst of his divorce. He felt he was having some kind of a delayed reaction and was losing his perspective. I was pleased when he told me he was working with a counselor, but my heart ached for him.

A week later, John and I talked while we watched Kaitlin ride miniature racecars. His doctor had put him on antidepressant and anti-anxiety medication, but panic and fear were still dominating his life. I tried to get him to focus on what a new life could be with those of us who loved him—his daughters, Alisa. I told him that, like me, he got all his pain at once. I also told him that when I was going through the worst time of my own divorce, a dear friend suggested that I develop a list of mantras I could recite whenever I felt myself sinking into panic. For two weeks during my lowest point, I told John, I'd had to say them every few hours just to stay in one piece. John didn't respond.

I studied my son with his close-cropped brown hair, his bushy brown mustache. He was still my handsome boy, but for the first time in my life I saw resignation when I looked into his brown eyes. I saw defeat. He hated his lack of control over the situation and his life. He was fearful that Michele was trying to reopen the divorce; he was very worried about the state of his finances; and, as always, he feared the impact of all this on Kaitlin and her future.

Again, I urged him to make his own list of mantras: the positive things in his life, his daughters, his hopes for the future, the strengths that would help him through, the many people in his life who loved him. I told him once again how much I loved him. I urged him to call me whenever he wanted—or needed—to talk. After that conversation I deepened my prayer for him. I had been praying for him all along, but now I prayed more and I prayed harder.

Shortly after his death, we found his list of mantras on the desk in his bedroom. They were hand-written on a San Jose Police Department report form:

- This will pass and I will be OK

- I can handle this

- Any anxiety I feel is just a reminder to use my coping skills

- It is only my thinking that makes me feel trapped, and I can change my thinking
- I have family who love and support me
- I have friends who love and support me
- I have a good job
- I love Alisa and Alisa loves me
- Kaitlin is going to be OK and she knows I love her
- Let it go
- I will be OK

He was trying so hard.

John called me on Election Day. Ordinarily we'd have talked politics, but not that day. The pain and defeat were clear in his voice. He said he was not doing well at work, didn't think he was being a good father to Kaitlin, and felt like he was dragging Alisa down. I told him I was sure he was doing his job well, that Donna and I had observed him being a loving and sensitive father to Kaitlin, and that Alisa's support was a natural gift in a loving relationship.

I suggested that it might be helpful to separate out the different issues that he was confronting and consider each one individually instead of lumping them all together. There was his sorrow and anger about the divorce, his anxiety over upending Kaitlin's life, his worry about finances, and his concern about dragging Alisa down.

"I started to have suicidal thoughts yesterday," John said abruptly. This was the first time he used the word "suicide." To reassure him I told him that during my own divorce, at my lowest point, I too had had suicidal thoughts. I never intended to act on them, but I'd been in so much pain I felt suicide was the one surefire way to make the pain go away. He assured me he was talking to his counselor about these suicidal thoughts. He also told me that, just to be safe, he had given his off-duty weapon to his friend Bruce.

My reaction to all this, rather than to panic, was to think he was doing everything by the book. He was seeing a counselor. He was talking and venting his feelings to me. He had given up his weapon. He was doing all the right things. This was John, my rock, and his nightmare would eventually have to pass. I didn't think about the fact that a cop has unlimited access to guns. And I knew nothing about cops, depression, and suicide.

I did know I couldn't stand how much he was hurting. I told him that I wanted to call him to check in every few hours. He told me not to hover, to stick to our regular Thursday night phone sessions, and that if he wanted to talk more often he'd call.

He called just a few days later, enraged because the realtor had finally found a buyer for the house he still owned with Michele, but she had refused to sign off on the sale. They owed more than the house was worth and would lose all their equity, but they could each at least walk away without any indebtedness. Michele was still hoping she could figure out a way to keep the house. John knew this was their last opportunity to unload the house without any future liability, and the window was rapidly closing. He told me, "I can't stand that I can't control this." He was completely frustrated by his powerlessness.

Later that week he was served with papers from Michele's new lawyer. She was attempting to reopen the divorce so the settlement could be changed; the papers also alleged a variety of financial misdeeds. He called me more distraught than I had ever heard him. I told him that he needed to hire his own attorney. I knew he was financially stretched, so I told him I would pay for it. Before he hung up he told me, "This will never end." I focused on managing the immediate problem, and I once more reassured him that this trying time would most certainly, eventually, come to an end.

He came up with Kaitlin the following weekend. I was waiting outside for them when John pulled up in the gray Honda pickup he'd purchased over the summer. He loved his new truck, though I liked to tease him about it. Kaitlin opened the passenger side and jumped into my arms. Then she ran up the front steps to see Grandma. John slowly got out of the truck and I mentioned that it was as ugly as ever. He smiled, but his eyes gave away his sadness. He looked utterly exhausted.

Grandma and Kaitlin went shopping after lunch. John and I took a long walk through the neighborhood and up to Mount Davidson, which looks east to downtown and the bay. John and I talked through everything once again: his sense of failure about the divorce, his concern about his parenting of Kaitlin, his anger at Michele, his frustration and regret about his financial situation and losing the house, what he should do to defend against reopening the divorce. I pointed out how each issue was manageable, how it would take some time, but that he would eventually come out in one piece.

I stressed that Donna, who spent a lot of time with Kaitlin, felt that she was handling her parents' divorce well—in part thanks to his parenting. Overall, Kaitlin seemed healthy and generally happy. That night, after Kaitlin went to bed, John and I talked some more and I wrote him a check to pay for his new attorney. He didn't want to take the check but reluctantly put it in his wallet. He knew he needed legal assistance.

Before John and Kaitlin got into the truck and drove away on Sunday, I hugged my son and held onto him for a long time. I wanted so much to take away his pain and distress. I knew that just as I had created a new life with Donna, he too would one day have a new life—with his daughters, perhaps with Alisa, and, as always, with me. Meanwhile, his suffering over the past months had left me worried and anxious about him. But he was my rock and I was his. He'd survive. It never once occurred to me that he wouldn't survive.

I headed to New York for a business trip and had dinner with my son Ed in the city. When I arrived home, on November 20, 2008, I immediately called John. He answered and said he couldn't talk. He was with his friend Bruce, whose marriage was also ending. He promised he'd call me over the weekend. The weekend came and went and he didn't call. I wanted to call him, but I remembered that he told me not to hover, so I played by the rules and didn't call. When I didn't hear from him on Monday or Tuesday I resisted the almost-overpowering urge to check in. It helped that at work I was buried in a last round of midyear Catholic Charities budget cuts as I prepared to turn the reins over to my successor in January. Before I knew it, it was Wednesday night and I hadn't had a real conversation with John in ten days.

Finally, on Thanksgiving morning, I called him on the pretense of asking what time he planned to bring Kaitlin to our house. She was going to stay with us while John and Alisa spent time in the city. At this moment John was with Alisa at Alisa's mom's house. In a low voice he told me he was feeling down. He said he didn't have time to talk, but they would drop Kaitlin off Friday evening and then return on Saturday night to grill some lobsters he caught on his last dive trip.

* * *

Here we are on the Saturday after Thanksgiving, 2008, on the deck again . . . John is "maintaining." Once again, we go over each issue he's confronting. John tells me he has made an appointment with his new attorney on Tuesday. I notice that his gestures and body movements have slowed, and I realize he is calm, without the anxiety that has plagued him relentlessly for the last two months. I don't understand what has brought on this sense of calm but it gives me some relief.

John grills the lobsters and we have a pleasant dinner. We discuss my upcoming retirement dinner the following Monday, and he confirms once again that he and Alisa will be there. "I wouldn't miss it," he tells me. Throughout the evening Donna has the growing intuitive sense that John is blaming himself for everything: the failed marriage, the financial trouble, the disruption to Kaitlin's life. Just before John and the girls leave, Donna takes him aside and tells him that marriages end all the time and no one party is ever to blame. She says that he shouldn't blame himself and reminds him that he's a wonderful father and is doing everything right. John thanks her but doesn't say anything more. I hug him and assure him yet again that he will come through this.

* * *

Ten months earlier I announced to the Board of Directors that I would soon step down as the executive director of Catholic Charities. I have spent over forty years in social services—most of that time, running large organizations—and am ready to do something less stressful. I plan to continue to volunteer at San Quentin. I am also excited about part-time teaching at the UC Berkeley School of Social Welfare, where I will focus on non-profit leadership training and the adoption of children from the foster care system. I assume, of course, that I am in control of my life and all will work out according to my plans.

My friend and former Board President of Catholic Charities, Clint Reilly, owns the Merchants Exchange Building, a San Francisco landmark. My retirement dinner is a going-away party for me but also serves as a fundraiser for Catholic Charities. Clint has given us the space free of charge in addition to donating all the wine for the evening. It is an elegant gala.

The Julia Morgan Ballroom is an architectural masterpiece that combines a timeless Beaux-Arts interior and superior modern amenities with an intricate gilded ceiling and redwood walls interspersed with massive floor–to–ceiling windows overlooking the city. The menu tonight starts with baby greens with goat cheese, pears, cranberries, and hazelnuts in balsamic vinaigrette dressing. The entree choices are pork tenderloin with spinach and wild rice or asiago cheese pasta with wild mushroom sauce and seasonal vegetables. The dessert is panna cotta in orange sauce.

The ballroom is packed with five hundred dinner guests, including my family, board members, staff, donors, the Archbishop of San Francisco, who is the Chairman of the Board, a number of priests and nuns with whom I worked over the years, other non-profit colleagues, city officials and many of my close friends. The men are in suits and ties and the women wear cocktail dresses or business suits. Donna is radiant in a powder-blue jacket and matching skirt.

John and Alisa are seated at our table, along with Donna and our daughter Danielle and my niece April and her fiancé, David. John is at my side the entire evening. In my mind's eye I see him sitting next to me. He looks tired and gaunt but seems to be enjoying himself, greeting my old friends as they come by the table to congratulate me. When one of the speakers extols my accomplishments at Catholic Charities, John rests his right arm on the back of my chair and whispers, "I'm not the only one who thinks you've done good work."

After a number of speakers sing my praises, it's my turn to get up and speak. I introduce Donna and Danielle, then look at my son and introduce John, my police officer, my firstborn, and my rock. I thank our board members, sponsors, donors and staff. I acknowledge colleagues, city officials and friends—especially Joe and Diane Harrington, who only days later will drop everything to be with me. I share my retirement plans, tell the audience what a privilege it has been to be the head of Catholic Charities, and thank them all for being there.

At the end of the evening, John and I are standing next to our table. He puts his arms around me and tells me how much he loves me and respects me. He kisses me on the cheek. As he's leaving he hugs Donna, strokes her hair, and tells her he loves her. This is the last time we'll ever see him.

Even with all the signs of John's increasing depression over the previous months, I don't have a clue where he is, though he sat next to me for hours at that dinner. Or maybe this particular evening I am so caught up in myself—basking in the praise of my friends and colleagues—that I simply don't pick up on how close he is to the end. It is only as I start to drift into sleep in the early morning hours that my worry and anxiety about John returns. Even then I only feel a familiar pang of what I've been dealing with over the last few months—pain because of John's pain. I have yet to learn what true pain really is.

Many pictures are taken that night—with board members and donors and staff, with family and friends, with colleagues and city officials. But when I think of that evening, only one picture comes to mind—a photo of John and me. John is dressed in a suit and tie, a very different look from his everyday attire. His arm is around my shoulder and we're both smiling as we stand near our table. I look at the picture every day. That moment—frozen in time in the photograph—was meant to represent joy and new beginnings and hope for the future. It has come to represent loss and heartache and shattered hope.

Donna hates this last picture of John because in it she can see the pain in John's eyes, and because it's likely that when it was taken John had already made the decision to end his life. But I can't hate the picture. It shows my last connection with John in this life—the last time I was with my rock.

* * *

On Tuesday, the morning after my retirement dinner, John takes Kaitlin to her counselor, who later states that he showed no signs of distress. On Wednesday he brings lunch to Alisa at her hospital during his break from work. They make a plan to have dinner at her place in Santa Cruz and he tells her he'll bring the wine. None of the officers on duty with him that day see anything unusual going on with him, beyond the signs he's been showing for months. John talks to one of his sergeants. The sergeant has been through a messy and costly divorce himself, and John asks him if things will get better. His sergeant assures him that they will. John checks out of work at 7:30 p.m. after helping a fellow officer with some paperwork. He already has the bottle of wine in his truck for his dinner with Alisa that night.

At ten Alisa calls me and tells me John hasn't shown up at her place. Later John's friend Bruce, a retired cop and neighbor, confirms that John's not in his own apartment, and then Bruce drives back and forth on Highway 17 in case John has gone off the road in the Santa Cruz Mountains on his way from San Jose to Santa Cruz. Bruce checks the local emergency rooms and a few hours later files a missing persons report in both Santa Clara and Santa Cruz counties.

I'm worried and I sleep fitfully, but I'm still in denial about what might have happened. I drive to Alisa's place early in the morning and Bruce joins us. I'm suppressing any possibility that John is dead. The worst-case scenario I can envision, or allow myself to envision, is John injured in his truck somewhere off Highway 17.

John is supposed to be at work at ten a.m. We call San Jose PD at ten fifteen and someone there says John is not at roll call. I call Donna at her childcare center and tell her. She'll tell me later that she collapsed in tears on the floor of her office after I hung up. She's getting ready to host a special event—opening a new library named after her best friend, who died earlier that year—but she leaves her office to drive down and be with me. Bruce and Alisa and I drive over to John's apartment in Scotts Valley. I'm still not facing reality.

We arrive at John's place at around eleven. At noon the doorbell rings. Bruce went outside a minute earlier when he saw a police car arrive. Now he comes in and stands in the hallway. He doesn't want me to hear this from a stranger. Behind him are the San Jose Deputy Chief, then John's Captain, then the chaplain, and finally the two officers who rode with John. Bruce gives me a long, anguished look. "John is gone," he says.

The men tell me that a hiker found John's body earlier this morning on a trail in Henry Cowell State Park. He shot himself sometime late last evening. His body lay there all night. His truck is in the parking lot. I'll find out later that the unopened bottle of wine is still sitting on the front seat.

2

I'm Just Trying to Breathe

WHEN I LOOK BACK on that horrific moment at John's front door when I learned that my son was gone, what I remember most are the business cards. Every single one of those San Jose Police Department representatives gave me a business card. They kept shoving them into my hands. Later I would realize how compassionate they were that day, but in the moment all I could think was, What am I supposed do with all these business cards?

I call Donna. She's already driving down Highway 280. I tell her to pull over. I tell her John is gone and his body has been found. She's gasping and crying, or maybe she was already crying when I told her to pull over. The SJPD officers who are here at John's condo offer to go up and get her, but Donna wants to get to me right away and she keeps driving. She stays in the outside lane and focuses on the car in front of her. She manages to keep her car steady, but her mind careens back and forth between horror and disbelief. She knows that she must get to me, that I need her to be with me.

I go out on the deck by myself. I can't feel my legs. I hold onto the railing. I'm having difficulty breathing. I don't know it at the time but I'm in shock; only when it wears off will I really experience the crushing pain of John's death and the way he died. Right now I'm feeling smothered and I'm just trying to breathe. On the deck in that moment I remember what Donna told John a couple of years ago, about his relationship to me. "You are your father's breath," she said, and it's as if this was literally true. Now I can't breathe.

I open my cell phone and start making phone calls. The hardest call is to Karen, John's mother. I have to tell her what happened to her son. She doesn't cry or sob but starts wailing. In that moment, standing on the deck and trying to breathe, I don't know what to say, and now I don't remember what I said. I don't remember what she said. I only remember the terrible wailing.

I call John's brother Ed in New York. I tell him. He says, "Dad, I can't imagine your pain. I'll be right out. I love you."

I'm still on the deck, holding onto the railing, still feeling like I'm being smothered. I'm thinking that if I can just start breathing again I can somehow get John back.

Donna arrives. I go back inside and we hold on to each other. Neither of us knows what to say so we just stand there in the living room, holding onto each other and crying. Then she starts calling family members. John's close friends come by: John Weiss, the Scotts Valley Police Chief, Steve Smith, Jim and Rene Keehn. Donna Lind, John's first Scotts Valley PD Sergeant, also stops by. She is the head of the Fallen Officer Foundation of Santa Cruz County and has her arms outstretched to us, a check ready for us to offset the funeral expenses.

The rest of that afternoon is a blur. Donna takes charge of calling the mortuary, making funeral arrangements, contacting the church—all the "death duties," as Joyce Carol Oates calls them in *A Widow's Story*. I am grateful for her assistance as I am deeply in shock.

That evening we go to Michele's to be with Krissy and Kaitlin. Michele greets us with a long, tearful hug, repeatedly saying, "I'm so sorry." We walk into the living room and hug the girls. Donna, holding Kaitlin, is flooded with her own memories of losing her mother when she was eight. She quietly tells Kaitlin about that. Kaitlin holds on to her but doesn't say anything. Kaitlin will learn in a few days how her dad died, but right now isn't the time to tell her. Instead Donna tells the girls how much their dad loved them and that we will always be their grandparents and will always be there for them. The girls are lethargic. I'm sitting there numb, useless.

Donna and I finally go back to John's place and collapse. That night I'm lying in bed. My beautiful boy, my rock, is gone. Donna comes in and quietly begins night prayers. Since early in our marriage, we've been practicing a shortened version of the Catholic Liturgy of the Hours; we make it part of our daily morning prayers and evening prayers. Tonight the reading is Psalm 62, which begins, "My soul rests in God alone. God alone is my rock and salvation . . . " It will be many months before any prayer gives me comfort, many months before I will become aware of how often in the Book of Psalms God is referred to as "our rock." I lie there, still feeling smothered, still trying to breathe. The horror begins to creep in. Donna holds me. This is the first of countless long nights to come.

On Friday we drive home, and Danielle is there to greet us. She is crying as she hugs me tight and tells me she loves me. We get some fresh clothes and immediately return to Scotts Valley. Later our dear friends Joe and Diane Harrington come down from Marin County. John's siblings, Ed and LeAnn, arrive. Ed graciously agrees to Donna's request to write John's obituary. In the last six months of John's life Ed had reached out to him twice but John never responded. As I look back I realize how difficult it must have been for Ed to write that obituary and what an act of love it was. We decide that John will be cremated and that part of his ashes will be taken to the ocean where he loved to dive, and part will be taken up to the mountains where he and I spent so much time together. Much of this time is a blur, but somehow we decide to have the viewing on Sunday and the funeral on Tuesday morning.

* * *

On Saturday we go to the local Catholic Church—San Augustin—to make the Mass arrangements and select the readings and music. We meet with Father Jerry Maher, a young, personable Irish pastor. I tell him that my family is an eclectic mix of believers and non-believers and that I'd like them all to be comfortable with the funeral service. He suggests appropriate Mass readings. I'm too distracted in the moment to feel much of anything, but later I'll come to appreciate how well he helped us grieve John's death and celebrate his life.

I want to see my son before he is embalmed, so on Saturday afternoon we go to the mortuary in Santa Cruz. Donna waits in the lobby while I go into the viewing room to spend some time with John by myself. I walk up to the temporary casket and look inside, and that's when it hits me that this really has happened. He's gone. I'm not going to get him back. Part of his head is wrapped in a towel. He shot himself in the right temple but angled his gun slightly back so his face wasn't disfigured. I'll later learn that when he pulled the trigger his death was instantaneous, and he felt no physical pain.

I can't breathe, but as I stand beside the casket slowly my breath comes back and I begin to talk to John. I tell him that he is my beautiful boy, my rock, and my gift from God. I tell him that now he has the wisdom, joy, and peace that I always prayed he would have. I tell him I know he is with God. I want to believe that. That's what all believers say and think—isn't it? And I'm a believer. At least I think I am. But standing next to my son's casket, looking at his lifeless body, I'm overcome by the realization that even if he's with God, he is definitely, irreversibly, permanently not with me.

I tell John that I know he's no longer in pain. I want to believe that too. I tell him how much I love him. I tell him Donna and I will be there for Kaitlin and Krissy. I tell him how much I treasured the time I had with him.

I bend over and stroke his face. I want to embrace him, but the most I can do is place my arms across his chest and put my cheek against his cheek. I kiss him on the cheek the way I used to. I'm acutely aware that he is gone from this life, gone from my life—yet in this moment, in spite of the horror of his suicide and my clarity about his death, I feel close to him. I stroke his face again and again, because if I touch him I can stay connected to him.

In *My Son . . . My Son*, Iris Bolton, an Atlanta therapist, describes seeing her son's body on the operating table after he committed suicide: "I needed to touch him, to stroke his lifeless arm, to imprint the reality of his death on my brain, on my heart. I needed that moment to hold my son and say goodbye." I think I was trying to have it both ways—affirming the reality of John's death while at the same time trying desperately to keep him with me.

The worst time is late at night, that night and every night after that for a long while. Tonight, Saturday night, I'm wrapped in a suffocating mix of panic and despair. The most I can do is talk to John and say over and over, "My beautiful boy, my rock, my gift from God." Those phrases become my new mantras. Then I just hold on to Donna. I keep trying to breathe.

On Sunday we go to Mass at San Augustin. At the Consecration I usually pray, "My Lord and my God, if you wish, you can heal my children." Today, as the priest raises the host, I silently scream, Who are you? You didn't heal my son! You let him die! Why did you let him die? Why did you let him lose his way? How could you be so incompetent? You did *not* heal my son! After Mass I tell Donna. She points out that John is healed now, that he's no longer in pain, and that he's with God. Because Donna says it I don't reject it, but I don't understand what it means. I don't know what "with God" means. Right now I don't even know what "God" means.

Ever since I was a kid I'd had a simple, unexamined Catholic view of God and heaven—not questioning, not parsing, never having a reason to question or parse. When my natural mom died at age fifty-seven, I grieved that she didn't have a longer life, but because of her long illness I also felt some relief, for her, for my dad, and for myself. When my dad died I missed him terribly at first, but I was comforted by the fact that he'd lived a long and full life. In neither case did I spend much time thinking about where their souls went, comfortably assuming they were "with God," whatever that meant.

But now, as Donna and I drive home from church, I'm done with God for letting this happen. Donna is still trying to tell me that John is healed and with God. All I can think is that I wanted him to be healed before he put the gun to his head. I want John to be here, now, in this life. I want him to be with me, not with a God who could let this happen. It will take me quite some time to come around to what Donna is really trying to tell me that day.

C.S. Lewis, in his memoir about his wife's death, *A Grief Observed*, points out that religion, even for a believer, is not an immediate source of consolation. He writes: "Talk to me about the truth of religion and I'll listen gladly. Talk to me about the duty of religion and I'll listen submissively. But don't come talking to me about the consolations of religion or I shall suspect that you don't understand." Lewis goes on to write: "Not that I am in much danger of ceasing to believe in God. The real danger is of coming to believe such dreadful things about him. The conclusion I dread is not 'so there is no God after all,' but 'so this is what God's really like. Deceive yourself no longer.'" Lewis eventually made peace with God around the death of his wife, but for some time, in his rage after her death, he referred to God as the "Cosmic Sadist."

In *Making Toast*, Roger Rosenblatt's haunting memoir about losing his daughter, Rosenblatt writes, "A friend was visiting Jerusalem when he got the news about Amy. He kicked the Wailing Wall, and said, 'Fuck you, God.' My sentiments exactly."

Like Lewis and Rosenblatt, I don't question God's existence. But, also like them, I wonder how an all-powerful, all-loving God can be so neglectful, so uncaring and incompetent? But as Donna and I walk into John's apartment after driving home from church I realize that rage takes energy, and right now I'm too exhausted, depressed, and frightened to give God any ongoing attention.

That day we have the viewing for family, friends, and John's fellow officers. I want to be with John by myself again, so I go up to the casket. Even with the embalming, he looks like himself. I silently repeat what I told him yesterday. Donna comes up and stands next to me. She notices that there's a set of rosary beads in John's hands. Donna loves to pray the rosary, but she knows John wouldn't have had a clue what to do with the rosary beads. She whispers to me to take them out of his hands. Donna—full of love and intuition, my soul mate, my protector—is on the job. I remove the rosary beads and put them in my pocket. I spend another minute looking at John. I stroke his cheek. This time I'm even clearer about the fact that he's gone. I'm numb. I go and sit in the back and let everyone else have time with him.

That evening John's close friends from Scotts Valley PD and San Jose PD have a memorial gathering at Malone's, an Irish bar and restaurant in Scotts Valley. Donna and I are reluctant to attend, but the group is so warm and supportive, and it's clear how much they all love and respect John, that we decide to go. I give a brief toast to "Officer John Francis Cahill, my rock, and obviously a rock to many others." Then I stop and stand there silently in the middle of this crowd of John's friends. I know these folks are celebrating

John's life. That's what you're supposed to do when a loved one, a good friend, dies. But I can't. Not tonight.

Donna and I go back to John's apartment. This is our fourth night in this place. We're staying here because it's more convenient than making the hour-and-a-half drive back and forth to San Francisco. It never occurs to us to stay in a hotel, and at first we're too numb to consider the downside of staying here. I've been so despondent that I haven't even paid attention to where we are. I see the French country dining room set that John's mom Karen and I gave to John and Michele after our divorce. As I walk around the apartment I see John's pictures of Krissy and Kaitlin, of Alisa, of John and me on the top of Half Dome—my favorite picture of the two of us. On his bedroom wall I see a large, framed, topographical satellite map of the world. John loved this map, not just because it gave him perspective about his place in the world, but because it made him think about all the places in the world he wanted to see. In 2004 he visited his friend Steve Smith in Bosnia when Steve was training Bosnian police officers there. John told me that this was something he might do when he retired; he saw it as a chance to do some good, see the world, and have someone else pay for it.

I look down on the desk and see the check I wrote in mid-November for a new attorney, when Michele had hired her own attorney to reopen their divorce. He was supposed to meet with the attorney on the day before he died, but he cancelled the appointment. Sometime in the last few weeks of his life he had decided he wouldn't need to spend money on a new attorney. I remember when I gave him the check how I assured him that he would be successful in preventing the reopening of the divorce. I realize now that he couldn't hear that. And I remember him saying, "This will never end."

We go to bed at about one thirty in the morning, and it comes to me that we're in John's bed. Just a few days ago my son's living body lay here where I now lie. I am learning in so many different ways that he used to be here, but he's not here now. He's gone and I'm in his bed and the only thing left is the horror, the pain, the panic, and the shortness of breath. At first I think it hurts too much to be here—we should be in a hotel or at home in our own bed—but then I realize I won't be sleeping well anywhere, and all things considered I'd rather be close to where John used to be.

On Monday family and friends start to gather at the Scotts Valley/ Santa Cruz Hilton where Karen, Ed, and LeAnn are staying. Donna goes over there to be with Kaitlin and Krissy. I stay at John's place, writing in my journal, trying but failing to make any sense out of this, recording the facts but not understanding how this could have happened, how John could have done this, how he could be gone.

* * *

The next morning, December 9, we go to the mortuary before the funeral. I go up to the closed casket and talk to John one last time. I tell him how much I love him and how much I miss him and that Donna and I will look out for his girls. When I turn around I see my old friend Tim Norman, whose oldest son died as a military hero five years ago. I was there for Tim then, and he's here for me now. We hold onto each other and don't say a word because there's nothing to say.

As John's casket is carried outside, the San Jose PD Honor Guard and all the motor officers come to attention. Then, with twenty motorcycle officers in two columns leading the motorcade, we drive from Santa Cruz to San Augustin Church in Scotts Valley.

Our car is the first car following the hearse and Donna is driving. Later Donna will tell me that as we were driving up Highway 17 to Scotts Valley, she felt like the situation was so unbelievable it was surreal, not actually happening, more like a dream for her. But for me that moment—seeing the motor officers in front of the hearse, knowing the hearse is carrying John's body—is all too real. There's no escaping it. This is my son's funeral procession.

As we come up in front of the church, I see that there's a huge American flag hanging from a giant crane over the entire street. John Weiss arranged that, I'll learn later. We get out of the car. As the casket is removed from the hearse, the honor guard comes to attention and a SJPD officer begins to play *Going Home* on the bagpipes. I can't breathe and I can't feel my legs. We follow John's casket into San Augustin, Karen with Ed and LeAnn and me with Donna, Danielle, and Alisa. The church is packed, and there are fifteen priests standing on the altar—all friends, all in white vestments. I know that in addition to John's friends and fellow police officers, many of our friends are here. I keep my head down and hold on to Donna. This is the only way I can get some air and not crumble. When we get to the front we go over and hug Michele and the girls, who are seated in the front row. Later, at the Kiss of Peace during the Mass, we'll embrace all three again. We want our granddaughters and everyone in the church to know that we are focused on the girls and that we love them.

Rene Keehn, the wife of John's friend and neighbor Jim Keehn, reads the first reading from Chapter 3 of the Book of Wisdom: "The souls of the just are in the hand of God, and no torment shall touch them." Sitting in the church at my son's funeral, in spite of my shock and disbelief and horror, I take in these words. It dawns on me that John's torment is over. The image of John being in God's hands is a bit more tangible and accessible than what I usually think of when I hear the words "he's with God." It's even slightly comforting. But sitting in the pew, staring at my son's coffin, trying to breathe, I'm too numb, too shocked, and too horrified to grapple with anything transcendent. Nevertheless, for the slight comfort of those words from the Book of Wisdom, I'll always be grateful to Father Gerry Maher for suggesting this selection.

In the church that morning, I think that John was my rock and he loved me dearly, so how can it be that he's not here anymore? How could this solid, healthy, vibrant man suddenly be gone? For the first time, looking at his coffin, I realize how much I took John for granted, how much I took his love, his support, his companionship, his vibrancy—his very existence—for granted. In *Lament for a Son* Nicholas Wolterstorff writes, "The beauties of the familiar go unremarked. We do not treasure each other enough."

John's dear friend John Weiss, the Scotts Valley police chief, gives the eulogy for John, recalling their early years together as rookie cops and roommates. He describes John as a "cop's cop," a "consummate professional," a "skilled motor officer, and an accomplished scuba diver and hiker." He says John was "well-read, intellectually curious, well-travelled." He adds, "Beyond that mustache, close-cropped hair and officer presence was a generous and kind man." He describes John as a remarkable friend and a loving, devoted father to his daughters. He pauses and says, "Even the brightest and best souls among us lose their way." He concludes, "John's legacy is right here in this church, inside all of us." I feel some slight comfort, some connection to my John, listening to these words from my son's close friend.

The funeral Mass ends with a video of John's life created by his friend and former colleague, John Wilson from Scotts Valley PD. The video is ten minutes long. I sit there, still holding on to Donna, still trying to breathe, watching my son's life pass before me from infancy until last week. I want to slow the video down, want it to be just the first segment of my son's story. All too soon the video is over. John's life is over. I feel like his life has only been ten minutes long.

Outside the church the honor guard comes to attention and again the bagpiper plays, this time *Amazing Grace*. I'm presented with the crucifix and the American flag that were on John's coffin. I'm standing there, holding onto the crucifix and the flag, numb. Surrounded by family, friends, John's friends and uniformed cops, I can't breathe.

When we get back to John's place that night we're exhausted but we can't sleep. Donna opens our prayer book and finds the night's evening prayers. Her eyes fall on the introductory psalm, Psalm 31. She pauses, looks at me, and reads, "You are my rock and my refuge . . . " All I can think of is that my rock is gone.

I doze off a few times, and each time I wake I have a few seconds before I realize John is gone. And then I think of how much anguish he felt at the end, and how much I miss him, and how it couldn't have happened, and how it did happen, how I let it happen, and how much it hurts.

I get up, go out to the living room, and pick up the picture of the two of us on Half Dome. The picture was taken in late September 2002, half a decade before John's marriage fell apart, before John lost his way. If I could have only one picture of John, it would be this one. Another climber took it for us as we were standing side by side on the edge of the cliff.

That day John and I started hiking up the Mist Trail at the floor of Yosemite Valley. Half Dome is 4800 feet straight up, but you have to hike eight miles on steep trails to get there. We climbed a trail of granite steps to the top of Nevada Falls, and then did another steep hike to the top of Vernal Falls. We were climbing next to the plunging water as it sprays off the granite. Had it been spring we would've been soaked, but that day we were covered in a fine mist that cooled us as we climbed. John periodically stopped along the way, ostensibly to take pictures but actually to give me a break. After the falls, we headed east through Little Yosemite Valley.

Then the real work began. The last two miles were mostly switchbacks, more steep granite steps, and then a long steep section of loose rock. At this point, shortly before we came to the final 400-foot cable ascent, I was winded and dehydrated and my legs felt like jelly. John told me that we didn't have to keep going, but I reminded him that we'd already bought the "I Got to the Top" tee shirts, so we had to. Without saying a word, he reached back, grabbed my belt buckle and pulled me up the trail.

Later he would tell his friend Bruce that he realized in that moment that after years of me taking care of him, he was now, for the first time in his life, taking care of me. I remember what a strange and wonderful feeling it was for John to be pulling me up the trail.

By the time we got to the cable ascent I was feeling better. This last part of the climb is steep, but having the cables to grab onto made it relatively easy. It was more dangerous than strenuous, and a number of folks have slipped off the cables and lost their lives. John had me go up the cables first so he could stay behind me.

We got to the top of Half Dome, 8800 feet above sea level. The view was stunning. We could look down to the floor of Yosemite Valley and the Merced River. We could look southwest over to Glacier Point. We could look north in the direction of Hetch Hetchy, where I would spread John's ashes seven years later.

We took an hour's rest before we started back down, not just because I was sixty-two years old but because I wanted to stretch out this time with my son on this beautiful piece of God's creation. I was on top of the world with my son. We talked about the ups and downs of marriage. We talked about the joys and challenges of fatherhood. We soaked up the beauty and each other's presence. We didn't know this would be our last serious trek together.

In the picture we're standing six feet from the edge of the cliff that drops almost a mile to the valley floor behind us. Behind us, on the other side of the valley, are sheer granite slabs interspersed with groves of pine trees below a bright blue sky and three white clouds. John has his right arm around my shoulders. We're both in hiking shorts. John has on a blue windbreaker and I'm in a blue fleece zip-up jacket. We're both wearing baseball caps, and our faces are partially shaded. We have small smiles on our faces, not the kind of huge smiles where you want to tell the whole world how happy you are but rather understated looks of fulfillment, contentment, quiet joy—looks that give no hint of what is to come.

* * *

The Half Dome photo triggers a flood of memories. I met Karen as I was finishing my active duty in the Marine Corps Reserve, and we married in 1965. John was born in 1966, Ed in 1967, and LeAnn in 1969. I went from the seminary to the Marine Corps to marriage. I was no more prepared to be a husband and father than I was to be an astronaut. In the years to come I would fail early on to spot my daughter's depression. I would fail to make my son Ed feel loved and protected, especially as he was questioning his sexuality. And of course, in the end, I would fail to protect John.

But what I lacked in self-awareness and maturity as a young man, I made up for with unbridled optimism. I remember a picture of John and me, taken by Karen in our living room in the spring of 1967. John was a year old and not quite walking. In the background, at the top of steps leading down to the front door, is a wooden gate Karen and I installed to keep John from crawling down the stairs. A few days earlier John had gone through the gate, which was closed but—unknown to us—unlocked, and John started to tumble down the steps. Karen screamed, and she and I both raced to the top of the steps. Karen was six months pregnant, so I beat her to the gate, flew down the stairs, and caught John on the landing halfway down. He was crying but unhurt. At the time this picture is taken, the gate is safely locked. John is in a green tee shirt and green-striped coveralls. He's smiling and has his arms around my right leg. He looks very happy to be holding on to his dad. I have a small grin on my face, perhaps still feeling a little guilty about the unlocked gate, but secure in the knowledge that I will always be able to protect and rescue my children, no matter what happens.

John and I were kindred spirits, especially when it came to backpacking and fishing. In July of 1978, when John was twelve, he and I arrived at O'Shaughnessy Dam in northern Yosemite for a camping and fishing trip. We put on our backpacks for a six-mile hike around the far side of Hetch Hetchy Reservoir to Rancheria Creek, where there are usually plenty of rainbow trout. All the kids learned to fish while we camped every summer on the Middle Fork of the Tuolumne River, but John was the most patient and persistent. I would take him for day trips to Cottonwood Creek, which ran into the Tuolumne. We would work the stream for hours within sight of each other, not talking but completely connected.

One long-ago day on our way to Rancheria Creek, our backpacks hold all our normal gear for a three-day trip—plus some steaks for the first night, a large roll of salami, a brick of cheddar cheese, some oranges, and granola bars. Because John is only twelve I carry most of the weight. All he can think about is getting there to start fishing. We arrive at the creek after a hot, dusty hike alongside the reservoir. John drops his pack, rigs up his fishing rod and takes off for the stream. I drop my pack, take a drink of water, and head upstream to look for a good campsite.

All of a sudden I hear a loud noise where we left the backpacks. I come back downstream, and I see a very large brown bear and her two cubs beginning to tear through our backpacks. I dart in to try to grab the packs, but the mother goes up on her hind legs and roars at me. I back away. John comes back from the stream. We stand there, about twenty yards away, and watch the bears enjoy two New York steaks, a large salami roll, wrapper and all, the cheddar cheese, the oranges, skin and all, and for dessert, the granola bars. The bears finish dining and leave us to our misery. We hike the six miles back to the dam, our backpacks in shreds, tired, hungry and disillusioned campers. Over the years John and I would do a number of backpack trips, never forgetting to hang our packs, but we'd always look back on this trip, remembering how much the bears of Rancheria Creek enjoyed the meal we served them.

I remember John's four years of high school soccer. I never missed a game. And I remember the day he borrowed my newly-painted Datsun pickup truck to drive to the store for something. He leaves the store, gets in the truck and puts his money on the seat beside him. The windows are open. He starts up the truck and drives away. The cash starts flying around inside the cab of the truck. John tries to grab the cash and steer the truck at the same time. He drives off the road onto the shoulder. Then he veers left, crossing over the yellow line almost to the other shoulder. He swerves back to the right, only this time the truck tips over on its side, sliding down the middle of the road. John wasn't injured, but my truck was. I remember not being surprised that John was unhurt. I simply assumed that he wouldn't be hurt. I took it for granted that he would never be hurt.

* * *

Before he graduated from college John decided he wanted to be a police officer. I knew there were risks with the job, but I was proud of his career choice. John's first job as a cop was in a small town in the Santa Cruz Mountains, at the Scotts Valley Police Department. Later he transferred to the San Jose Police Department. When he started at Scotts Valley PD he made some new good friends. John Weiss was a fellow rookie cop and John's first roommate. Cahill and Weiss were close friends from the beginning, not just enjoying their freedom as young, beer-loving bachelors but also sharing a curiosity about the world around them. John Weiss was a lot more than just a cop; he was a writer, an artist, and a clever cartoonist. John Cahill loved fast motorcycles and scuba diving. Cahill and Weiss developed a lifelong trust and affection for each other. Later John roomed and became friends with another fellow officer, Steve Smith, with whom he shared a love of world travel. John also became close with Bruce Lindsay, a Scotts Valley cop who was a fellow scuba diver. Bruce was a few years older than John, with a healthy dose of cop-like cynicism about bureaucracies and other aspects of the working world. After Bruce's marriage ended he moved into the same condo complex John was living in. Toward the end, Bruce and John spent a lot of time supporting each other.

* * *

In late 1995, my dad died. Shortly after that my daughter LeAnn, struggling with depression, began to pull away from me. LeAnn would come back into my life after John died, but then she would pull away again. In May of 1996 the newly-elected mayor of San Francisco replaced me as the head of the Department of Social Services. A few months later Karen and I ended our marriage.

In September John helped me move out of the house I shared with Karen into a one-bedroom apartment. I was working for a consulting firm, helping state governments develop their child welfare services. I appreciated having the work, but I hated being on the road, and after losing my dad, my marriage and my daughter, I was depressed. One day, on the morning plane to Seattle from San Francisco, I realized I would be fine with it if the plane went down. And once during that time, standing on a trail that looks out over the Golden Gate Bridge, I thought of how a few months ago a man had committed suicide by going off one of the nearby cliffs; and I understood for the first time how someone could feel so much pain, could feel so depressed, could feel so lost, that they could end their life. Later on I would find out that suicidal thoughts are not an uncommon reaction for people who have had the bottom torn out of their lives. Eventually I would find out a lot more about suicide.

Ed hosted me back east for Christmas at Rutgers, where he was working on his doctorate. He lovingly took care of me for four days. Ed would go on to teach English at Fordham University in New York and eventually begin his life with Mark, a novelist and screenwriter. During the next few months John became my rock, talking with me regularly on the phone, taking long walks with me, having me down often for dinner, telling me how proud he was of the way I was handling things, and reminding me that I would survive, just as I would later remind him, when he went through his divorce, that he would survive.

Later I met Donna. She was a single mom with an eleven-year-old daughter, Danielle, and was about to become the executive director of Holy Family Day Home, the oldest early childhood education program in San Francisco. John and Michele made Donna feel welcome and accepted. In September Michele gave birth to Kaitlin Leigh Cahill. I was happy, I was in love, and I had a second granddaughter.

Donna and I were married in July 1998, and John was my best man. At the reception John gave the wedding toast, "To my father—my teacher, my hero, and my fellow backpacker—and to Donna, who has brought joy to my dad." Now, as I sit in John's dark living room, I can see John standing on the stage in the parish hall of St. Teresa's Church, giving the toast. I remember how proud of him I was, how grateful I was for his love, his friendship, his support—my first-born, my fellow backpacker, my beautiful boy—my rock.

For my sixtieth birthday, on September 10, 2000, Donna rented the banquet room at Delancey Street, one of our favorite restaurants, and Donna, Danielle, my mom Ruth, and some of our close friends came. John drove up with Krissy and Kaitlin. After dinner he gave the toast. There's a picture of him making the toast, with me standing next to him. In the picture I'm trying not to cry as he's telling the group how much he loves me and how much he respects me.

That evening, as I looked at my wife, my son, my family, and my friends, I realized how blessed I was, how happy and grateful. I also had just been appointed as the executive director of San Francisco Catholic Charities. I thought of what my dad used to say when he was happy and grateful: "Deo

Gratias," thanks be to God. I remember thinking as John toasted me that night that my son would be around to toast me on my seventieth birthday, and on my eightieth birthday if, God willing, I was still around.

* * *

It's five in the morning and I'm still wide-awake, sitting in the living room of John's apartment. The memories can't stop the horror from coming back. The memories are no match for the perverse unnaturalness of a father out-living his son. In *Stations of the Heart*, Richard Lischer writes about his son's death from cancer: "There is no word in western language for the parent of a dead child."

3

I Will Choose to Honor My Son

THE NEXT DAY WE clean John's place and pack up. Our friend Diane Harrington, who knows we're stressed, in shock, and haven't eaten or slept much, urges us not to go home right away, but take a couple of days to be by ourselves. We drive up to Sebastopol in Sonoma County, where we've cut down our Christmas tree every year for fifteen years. Cutting down a Christmas tree seems obscene to me now and is the last thing I want to do, but Donna knows that we need to rest and, at least for a short time, focus on something else.

We crash for the night at a bed and breakfast inn where Diane made reservations for us. I wake up at around five in the morning. I'm crying, but Donna is asleep and doesn't hear me. In *The Long Goodbye*, Meghan O'Rourke writes about the impact of her mother's death: "Waking up in a world without her is like waking up in a world without sky: unimaginable." For me, waking up in a world without John is like waking up in a world without air.

I silently say my new mantras: "My beautiful boy, my gift from God, my rock, my anonymous Christian." I tell John I know (I hope) that he is with his grandparents, Margaret and Everett; with Karen's parents; and with his namesake, his great-grandfather, John Carl Cahill.

I'm lying there wide-awake, thinking I should get up and go get a newspaper. But I have no interest in the news and no desire to read any newspaper or magazine, nor do I care what's going on in the world. I was a nightly CNN junkie all through the 2008 presidential campaign, but on Election Day, while I was pleased that Obama won, I was more focused on John's pain and depression. Now, a month later, politics and elections are irrelevant. I'm sure that whatever life is in front of me will not involve CNN, *Time* magazine, and the *New York Times*.

And then I hear John speak to me: "Dad, you have to live your life and do the things you planned to do, so you have to stay informed." It's not an external voice that I hear, but I know with total clarity that I'm not imagining it. This won't be the last time I'll hear John. In *Meditations for Survivors of Suicide*, Joni Woelfel writes about hearing her son, who had also taken his life: "One day, I was trying to make a decision about a problem, and I heard Mic's voice in my mind say, 'Mom, it'll be fine,' the way he always said those words with such enduring friendliness." That is how I hear John in my mind: clear—not conjured, not imagined. I'm too numb to focus on the implications, but I'm pretty sure this is really John, that somehow he is actually, truly talking to me. After Donna wakes up I tell her about hearing John. She looks at me and smiles. "I'm not surprised," she says softly.

Also at our friend's suggestion, Donna has arranged for each of us to get a massage that afternoon. When she told me this I thought it was even more obscene than cutting down a tree, but again, she insisted. Donna informed the spa staff about John ahead of time, and from the moment we walk through the spa door everyone is incredibly sensitive and compassionate. As soon as I get under the sheet on the massage table and rest my head in the frame I start to cry.

Then it happens again: I hear John's voice. "Dad, it's a massage! Relax. Enjoy it." Just the way John always sounded when he was giving me advice, mildly condescending and full of affection and concern. So I do what I'm told. I take slow, deep breaths and stop resisting the masseuse as she tries to work the tension out of my shoulders and neck. I fall asleep for a few moments and in the instant after I wake up I still feel that John has been looking out for me. But then I'm back in reality, and I know he's gone. Later, Donna and I take a walk around town, have an early dinner and try to get some sleep.

The next day we cut down our tree at the Garlock Christmas Tree Farm, where we have been coming for years. Donna talks to Becky Garlock, one of the owners, and tells her about John. Becky looks at me, puts her arms around me and says, "I'm so sorry. I can't imagine losing one of my children." Then, with a tearful smile, she says, "But I'm glad Donna brought you up here today." It would be months before I would appreciate Becky's response—a natural, honest expression of love and support, with none of the understandable awkwardness that is evident in some folks when they learn about my son's death.

After we tie the six-foot Douglas Fir to the top of our car, we go to a nearby apple ranch where each year we buy apple juice and apple bread, then stop for dinner on the way home. I know that Donna is trying to distract me with this little trip, but I'm numb, not even able to process the fact that I've heard John speak to me, or what he said, much less appreciate the natural kindness and warmth of Becky Garlock.

When we get home that night I still can't sleep. I get in the shower about midnight and stay there until the hot water runs out, as I will do most nights for the next six months. Then I get into bed and do my mantras.

The next morning, Saturday, I open my top dresser drawer to get some socks. Off to the side is the birthday card John had sent me in September. "Dad," he wrote on it, "I love you, and you have been my 'rock' this year. I am so proud to be your son." As I look at the card now, at his handwriting on it, I don't feel that I've been his rock, especially at the end.

In the shower that night I tell John that I know we were connected when he was alive, and I hope we'll still be connected now. I hear John say, "Dad, we were always connected. Now we're connected in a different way." This is the first time I hear John in the shower. I have the same certainty that it's him, that I'm not imagining this. It's comforting, but it doesn't make the pain go away.

Donna and I go to Sunday Mass. The response to one of the readings is, "My soul rejoices in God." My soul is not rejoicing anywhere, and definitely not in God.

* * *

That afternoon we drive down to John's place to begin putting his affairs in order. Alisa has left us a beautiful note thanking us for supporting her and including her. The next time I see her I tell her that supporting her came naturally, because all I have to do is think about losing Donna eight months after I met her to know what Alisa's experiencing.

Through the end of January I'll go down to Scotts Valley for a few days every week and get as much done as I can. Dealing with life insurance, pension, real estate, college funds, probate, and income tax issues will turn out to be almost a year of steady work, but eventually it proves to be a distracting hedge against full-time depression.

A week after the funeral, we pick up John's ashes at the mortuary. They're in two separate, thick, cardboard containers, one for the mountains and one for the ocean. I walk out of the mortuary holding the ashes of my first-born, an act that is so beyond the imaginable, so incongruous, so horrifying, so unreal. Part of me knows that I'm holding what's left of my son in my hands. Another part of me remains separate, out of my body, an observer of some other father's tragedy, some other son's ashes.

Donna has bought a light yellow and gray box with the words, "Faith, Hope, Love" printed on the lid. She places the two cardboard containers inside the box. She also purchases two silver lockets and places a small amount of John's ashes in each of them to save for Krissy and Kaitlin.

The next morning Donna reads morning prayers, which include Psalm 34: "The Lord is close to the brokenhearted, and those who are crushed in spirit He saves." Brokenhearted and crushed, absolutely. But I don't know about the rest of it.

* * *

On the afternoon of December 20 I bring up the Christmas decorations from our garage, and Donna begins to decorate the tree. I have no enthusiasm for this project, so Donna is doing most of the work, stringing the lights and hanging the ornaments. At six thirty the doorbell rings. I open the door and a woman in her late thirties is standing there. She's average height, has dark brown hair, and is wearing a long gray raincoat. She looks tired, as if this is her last stop for the day. "Brian Cahill?" she asks. I nod and she cheerfully tells me she's delivering a document from Santa Cruz County Superior Court. She hands me an envelope, and I feel a knot in my stomach form. She keeps smiling, maintaining her cheerful demeanor. I'm standing there thinking that there is no logic in a process server being cheerful unless it's some kind of self-protection.

Thanking her seems inappropriate, so I nod again and close the door. I open the envelope, still standing there in the front hall, and take out a thick document. It's notice of a lawsuit filed by Michele's attorney, officially informing me as executor of my son's estate that she is reopening her divorce from John. I hand the document to Donna in the living room. She reads the first page and looks at me, stunned. I'm stunned too. This is not what we expected five days before Christmas and less than two weeks after John's funeral.

I move some of the ornament boxes off the dining room table and sit down and review the entire document. Not only does it seek to reopen the divorce, it also includes financial allegations against John, an effort to claim part of John's estate, and a petition to file her action against me in place of John, because I'm the administrator of the estate with control over John's life insurance and retirement funds. My head is throbbing when I finish reading, and I hurl the document on the floor. I'm ready to explode.

A few times, at my last two jobs, the agencies I worked for were sued; now I think about how I geared up for battle and went to war with whoever was trying to hurt our organization. I tell Donna that if Michele wants to go to war, I'm up for it. Donna is still stunned and doesn't respond. Later I will come to realize that Michele was acting on her attorney's advice, and she was frightened by her own financial insecurity. But right now all I can think is, Okay, I know how to do this. If someone wants to mess with my son, I'm ready to fight back. Then, as I reach down to pick up the document, I realize that I'm not going to have the opportunity to grieve for John without other painful distractions.

That night Donna and I watch the DVD that John's friend, John Wilson, made about the life of his friend John Francis Cahill. Donna and I saw the video at the funeral, of course, but we decide to watch it again now. I'm the one who wants to see it again. Donna's not so sure that we should watch it—that I'm ready to watch it—but I have to, because it's a way to be connected to him, a way to get him back, a way to hold on to him. I have to see him in my arms when he is a week old. I have to see him with his arms wrapped around my leg when he's a year old. I have to see him scoring a goal from midfield in his junior year. I have to see him on the scuba diving boat, on the white water raft, on his SJPD motorcycle. I have to see him hugging Krissy in her pajamas in the garage and kissing Kaitlin while he's kneeling on the grass. I have to see him standing with me on the top of Half Dome. And, I don't want to, but I have to see him at my retirement dinner, standing with his arm around me. I sit on the sofa crying, Donna next to me, holding on to me. It hurts, but I have to watch it. I have to be connected. Meghan O'Rourke, writing about the weeks after her mother's death, says it all: "I wanted her back so intensely, I didn't want to let go."

I go to bed, depressed and exhausted, but I'm not able to sleep. I finally give up and get in the shower. I don't hear John. The hot water runs out. After I'm out of the shower I get on the scale. I've lost twenty pounds in sixteen days.

* * *

I've been dreading the holidays, and now, a few days later, Christmas Eve is unavoidably here. It's around noon and Donna is beginning to prepare for our family dinner. I'm at the sink doing my regular non-skilled job of peeling potatoes. I usually don't like this chore, but today, alternating between numbness and despair, wanting to skip the whole Christmas routine, I'm pleased to have something I can focus on that's tangible, that's doable, that I can control, that doesn't cause pain.

In the evening my cousin Joan arrives with my mom Ruth. Krissy drives up with Kaitlin from Scotts Valley, and Danielle gets home from work. The Cahill family, such as it is, sits down for Christmas Eve dinner. Donna says grace because I can't. I can't be grateful for anything. I can't bless anything. As Donna finishes grace she comes to the words, "the souls of the faithful departed" and I realize she is talking about John, my son who is "departed," and I can't breathe. We have our meal, trying to keep the conversation light, not acknowledging the monstrous change that took place in our lives three weeks ago. Later, we open presents, but I'm so aware of John's absence this Christmas, and that he will be absent during every future Christmas and every other future holiday, and not only holidays but every day forever, that I can't pay attention to what's going on. I'm such a mess I can't even focus on what my granddaughters must be feeling.

I wake up Christmas morning, thinking this is a good day to stay under the covers. Donna's already in the kitchen with Danielle, and I can hear them quietly talking. I get up, put on my robe, and go out to the kitchen. Donna kisses me and pours me a cup of coffee. Danielle is chopping an onion on the counter next to the sink. She turns around and announces that she's cooking Christmas brunch for me. Then she wipes off her hands and gives me a long hug, not saying anything, just holding me. I've learned over these last few weeks that my stepdaughter—the twenty-three-year-old woman I think of simply as my daughter—always knows when I need a hug, even when she's in a different part of the house. I stand there holding her, not surprised. She has her mother's intuition. She's also a great cook, and she produces a delicious bacon, cheese, onion, avocado, and tomato omelet. I sit around the island counter with my wife and daughter, enjoying the excellent meal, aching for John but feeling the love of these two women.

A few days later we're in John's apartment continuing our work tying up his affairs. Donna finishes packing John's dishes, glasses, and silverware, then she leaves to go pick up Kaitlin. Bruce comes by. He has no particular reason to be here, but it's clear he's really feeling John's loss and needs to talk about it. I sit on John's bed. Bruce sits sideways on the chair in front of John's desk. There's a picture of John on the left-hand corner of the desk. It shows him wearing a short-sleeved sport shirt and jeans, standing at the base of a waterfall in a grotto. He was in Bosnia then, visiting Steve Smith who was there training police officers. Bruce keeps glancing from the photo to me. Slowly, painfully, he starts telling me about how much John helped him when he, Bruce, was struggling with his own divorce. I look at him and see how hard it is for this tough cop to express his feelings, how much he misses his friend. I'm reminded that I'm not the only one grieving.

* * *

On Monday I receive a call from one of my board members, a long-time friend and colleague who lost a daughter some years ago. Rita tells me that I'll feel the pain and loss of John's death every day for the rest of my life, and I'll have no choice about that. But she says I do have a choice in front of me, and that is whether to retreat from life or to live the rest of my life in honor of my son. I'm feeling the urge to retreat, to stay under the covers, to stay in the shower, to hide from the world, so it will take some time before her message sinks in. And it will take some time before I realize how I can honor John.

Later, when I read Iris Bolton's beautiful and painful book about her son's suicide, *My Son . . . My Son,* I'll be struck by the poem she wrote and used as a preface:

> I don't know why.
> I'll never know why.
> I don't have to know why.
> I don't like it.
> I don't have to like it.
> What I do have to do is make a choice
> about my living.
> What I do want to do is to accept it and
> go on living.
> The choice is mine.
> I can go on living, valuing every moment
> in a way that I never did before,
> or I can be destroyed by it and,
> in turn, destroy others.
> I thought I was immortal.
> That my family and my children were also.
> That tragedy only happened to others.
> But I know now that life is tenuous and valuable.
> So I am choosing to go on living,
> making the most of the time I have,
> valuing my family and friends in a way never possible before.

Eventually, over the next year, it will come to me that I, like Iris Bolton, can choose to go on living, to make the most of the time I have—and that my way of doing that will be helping other cops avoid what happened to John.

I head for a weekend retreat at the Jesuit Retreat Center in Los Altos, something I've been doing annually for the last few years. During the retreat I spend my time praying, or at least trying to pray, walking, talking to John, and reflecting on everything that's happened. At Mass that night, after com-munion, I hear, "I am with you, Dad." Again, I'm comforted, but I still want to tell him that he's not with me the way I want him to be with me. I want to walk with him, to talk with him, to hug him, to tell him I love him, to comfort him, to tell him that he can come out of this.

I have a conference with Father Bernie Bush, a veteran Jesuit coun-selor and retreat master and the wisest priest I know. Bernie is a tall, lanky seventy-five-year-old with fading red hair. He was on the altar for John's funeral Mass. I walk into his office and he gives me a hug. "I'm glad you're here." I look at him. "I guess if one is pissed at God and in a shitload of pain, a retreat center is not a bad place to be," I say. He nods and my eyes start to fill with tears. "I really don't understand why God allowed this. John's suicide, his so losing his way, makes no sense at all, and I continue to want to scream at God and ask him what the hell he was thinking."

Bernie lets me calm down and then he tells me that when we ask God why, the only answer we can get is "because I love you." I look at him and say, "That's it, that's all there is? That's the only answer we're going to get?"

"You won't get any more until eternity, but you might get some graces from your loss before then," he answers.

It is only because I respect him so much I don't walk out. It will be a long time before I understand that he is right about the graces that come out of this kind of loss.

Iris Bolton writes about what her psychiatrist friend told her after her son shot himself: "You have no reason as yet to believe what I am going to tell you, but I ask you to hear me with an understanding heart. There is a gift for you in your son's death. You may not believe it at this bitter moment, but it is authentic and it can be yours if you are willing to search for it. To other eyes it may remain hidden. The gift is real and precious and you can find it if you choose." Bolton took a while to figure out what the gift was, where to look for it and find it. I'll take much longer.

* * *

As I'm walking around the retreat center property I come to a memorial plaque for Tom Petrini, a San Francisco deputy police chief who took his life in the 1990s. I was not a personal friend of Tom's, but I worked with him when I was running Social Services and I had great respect for him. I remember thinking when he died that what happened to him would never happen to John. I stand there wondering if Tom and John have gotten to-gether by now in some special first responders section of heaven.

That night I sit in the chapel crying. "I put my trust and my pain in your hands," I say to God. But putting my trust and pain in God's hands won't prove to be an ongoing commitment. At best it will be a one-time, short-term deal, something I have to do every day. I still have to do it every day.

* * *

The next day when I'm home, I notice one of John's death certificates sitting on my desk. I've been avoiding doing this, but now I pick up the document and slowly begin to read. In section 107 the cause of death is listed as "gunshot wound of the head." It seems to me that it should read "gunshot wound *to* the head." Instead of a line for the date of death, there's a line for "date of event." I now feel and will always feel that the word "event" does not refer to a picnic or a ballgame, or a fundraiser, or a wedding or a christening or an anniversary, or even a funeral. The word "event" has only one definition, one meaning and one context. It's only about John Francis Cahill and what he did to himself, his death—his "event."

The certificate shows the date as December 4, because that's when John's body was found. But I'm pretty sure John didn't sit out there on that trail all night, so for me, his last day in this life was December 3.

There's a section 112 for "other significant conditions contributing to death but not resulting in the underlying cause given in 107." The response reads, "depressive reaction by history." I have two reactions to this. I'm pretty sure John's depression was an underlying cause in his shooting himself. But I also want to go down to the coroner's office to set the record straight and tell them that John's "depressive reaction" was only in the last eighteen months; it was not "by history." I want to walk through the office telling all the staff people there that my son, for the greater part of his life, was vibrant, healthy, and secure. He loved being a cop. He loved motorcycle riding and backpacking and scuba diving and traveling, and he loved Krissy and Kaitlin and Alisa and me.

* * *

In between Christmas and New Year's my niece April and her fiancé host a long luncheon for Donna, Danielle and myself; for Ed and Mark who fly out from the east coast for the brunch and to spend a few days with us; and for LeAnn, Karen, Bruce, and Alisa. We watch family videos and tell endless stories about John. Everyone realizes that John has brought us together. John always wanted a large family around him. On this day his wish is fulfilled.

4

How Things Work With Cops

IT'S JANUARY 3, 2009. My son shot himself a month ago. I drive to John's apartment and let myself in. The place is quiet and still, and I think of all the times during the last year that I was here with John: having a beer with him, reflecting on the issues of the day, deciding where to go for dinner, asking how my granddaughters were doing, asking how he was doing. Now all I see is that his things are here but he is not.

I go through the rest of his files, including all his work-related documents, applications, training certificates, and performance evaluations. He was a good cop, strong and professional, but also sensitive and respectful. There is a consistent theme in the documents: John's willingness to treat people on the street with respect, which resulted in many tense situations being defused. Reading his evaluations now is another way to feel close to him. So I read them again. There's comfort in the confirmation of my own observation that over his years as a cop John never lost his humanity, was never racist, never abusive.

I remember a story he told me right after it happened, in 1997: He's on patrol with a younger partner and they're chasing a wanted felon through an east San Jose neighborhood. The guy they're chasing runs into a house. John and his partner ring the doorbell. A woman answers the door. She's the young felon's mother. She tells them he's in the back bedroom. John and his partner enter the bedroom. The man is under the covers pretending to sleep. John tells him to get up. The man explodes out of the bed, swinging a baseball bat. He hits John's partner on the side of the head and hits John on his left arm. John pulls out his baton and strikes the man on the back of his knees. John takes him down and cuffs him. A back-up officer shows up, looks at the younger officer's bleeding head and John's bruised arm and says, "I don't think you've questioned this guy enough. You should take five

minutes to question him more seriously and I'll wait outside." The suggestion hangs in the air that John and his partner should inflict on this guy at
least the same amount of pain he inflicted on them. The back-up officer
leaves. John says to his partner, "I don't feel any need to question this fool,
and if you have any brains you won't either." They leave with their prisoner
without any further "questioning."

Then I put away John's work files and open his closet. I'm struck by
how many pairs of boots are there. John was always acquiring the newest
state-of-the-art boots. All his boots are neatly laid out on the closet floor.
Most are hiking boots. Some are scuffed and well-worn; some still haven't
been totally broken in. There are a couple of pairs of brand-new work boots.
John liked to wear work boots with his jeans, and I used to tease him that
work boots should only be worn by guys who do construction work, and
that building things was not a skill possessed by John Cahill or his father
or his grandfather. I set aside the work boots for Donna's brother, knowing
that he can put them to good use. I take a pair of hiking boots for myself and
pack up the rest to donate to St. Vincent de Paul.

Next I move on to the books. Even though John lived in his apartment
for almost a year, he never unpacked most of his books, and they're still
in cardboard boxes against the wall next to his closet. I remove each book
slowly, holding it in my hand, wanting the book to connect me to John.
Some have his name written inside the cover. Some are history and some
are fiction, but many are on travel and exploration. One of the books was
a gift from John Weiss, and I find a card from Weiss among the pages. On
it he'd sketched a cartoon of John in uniform: square jaw, mustache, short
hair, and sunglasses. On John's nametag he wrote "God." In his note below
the cartoon he wrote, "Thank God I have you Cahill. You're the only one
in town I can talk to about the many important issues of the day. Happy
Birthday!" It was signed, "Johnny Weiss." I sit on John's bed crying, knowing
that neither John Weiss nor I will ever again get to talk about the important
issues of the day with John Cahill.

Later I go into the kitchen. I open the fridge and realize there's stuff in
there I'll have to take out and throw away. There's also a six-pack of New-
castle, John's favorite beer. I open one of the drawers next to the sink and
come across an old bone-handled bottle opener. The round metal end is
scratched and tarnished. The grooved, faded, ivory-colored handle is six
inches long and a half-inch in diameter, presumably the femur of a small
animal. One night after my dad retired he gave this bottle opener to me. I
was at his house having a drink with him and he was talking about his father. He looked at me and said, "I just thought of something." He got up and
went into the kitchen and I could hear him rummaging around in one of the

drawers. He came back into the living room with the opener. He said, "This was my father's. I want you to have it. Some day you can give it to John."

A few years ago, John was at my house and we were out on the deck drinking beer. We were both ready for a second one and I started to get up but he said he'd go. He came back with two bottles of Heineken and the bottle opener. He had never noticed it before, and he asked me about it. I told him it was my grandfather's, passed on to my dad and later to me. He handed it to me, but I decided on the spur of the moment to pass it on to him and gave it back to him. He loved it and told me he would keep up the family tradition and put it to good use.

Now, in John's kitchen on a gloomy winter day, I pick up the opener, holding it in my hand, knowing that John held it in his hand, knowing he'll never use it again. A lot of beer has been opened with this by four generations of Cahills. I'll give it to Ed, I decide.

In the shower that night, John's shower, I'm crying, feeling the panic and pain, telling John how much I miss him. I tell him that I know he's with God (this act of faith is still a work in progress) and that he is not in pain, but I miss him so much. I hear, "Dad, I am with God, I'm not in pain and I'll always be close to you." I take comfort in his words, in the fact that he is close and he is talking to me, but his death, his suicide, is still too horrific, too painful. Hearing him helps but it gives me no peace.

Joan Didion writes in *The Year of Magical Thinking*, "Grief, when it comes, is nothing we expect it to be. Grief comes in waves, paroxysms, sudden apprehensions that weaken the knees and blind the eyes and obliterate the dailiness of life." She adds, "Grief turns out to be a place none of us know until we reach it." I am just beginning to reach that place.

On the next night, January 4, I'm in my own bed, and I dream that John has something to do and I have to work his shift. I put on his uniform, but I realize I don't have his boots and I can't find the keys to his motorcycle. I can't do his job. I try, but I can't help him. When I wake up in the morning, I tell Donna about the dream. Usually Donna has to reflect for a moment before she tells me what she thinks is the meaning of some dream I've had. But now, sitting on her side of the bed, putting on her shoes and listening to me, she doesn't hesitate. She gently tells me that what strikes her as the point of the dream is to help me realize that I couldn't help John. I start to cry and tell her I was supposed to help him. I was his father. I was his rock. She turns to me, smiles a sad smile, and says, "You did all you could to help him. No one could have prevented this. He made his own decision. And now he's with God." She reaches over, hugs me, and when it seems okay to leave me she goes into the bathroom to brush her hair. I'm still sitting on my side of the bed. It will be a long time before I come to accept that I wasn't able to help John. I think of the dream. If I could have just found his boots and his keys, I could've helped him.

An hour later I'm standing in the living room looking out the front window, thinking of John, thinking of the dream, still wishing I could've helped him. I see the mail carrier come by and drop off our mail. I go down to the garage and grab the packet of mail from the basket below the mail slot. I'm anxious to get some documents our lawyer is sending, and I bring the packet up and place it on the kitchen counter. There are some bills and a magazine, but no legal documents. Then I notice a small envelope addressed to me.

I open the envelope, hoping it's not another sympathy card. I want to be done with condolence notes and sympathy cards. We've gotten hundreds of them. This is a condolence note, but I relax as soon as I see who it's from: it's from Judy, and she knows what I'm going through. Judy is a friend and former colleague from Southern California who lost her son in a motorcycle accident in Mexico nineteen years ago. He was with his dad, Judy's former husband, when he died.

I remember when I heard about the accident. I did the best I could to support Judy then, but now, as I read her note—a message that's especially comforting because she knows what I'm going through—I realize I had no idea what she was feeling when she lost her boy. Did she have difficulty breathing when she got the call? Did someone have to hold her up to stop her from crumbling as she walked into her son's funeral? Did she wake up every day and have a few seconds before she remembered he was gone? I was a good friend to her when she lost her son, but I didn't have a clue.

I put the note down on the kitchen counter. I think of my friend and wonder if it still hurts as much nineteen years later. I suspect it does. Then I think of John. He rode motorcycles all his life, at work and outside work. Would this hurt less if he had died in a motorcycle accident rather than from suicide? I suspect not. But standing in the kitchen so soon after losing John, I know, if I'm honest, I can't say for sure it wouldn't hurt less if he had died in a motorcycle accident. It's too soon to know the answer to that question. It hurts too much to pursue the thought. All I know is that John's gone.

* * *

I'm scheduled to go to Catholic Charities to continue cleaning out my office since I'm retiring. Donna knows that my staff will be at a loss for words, so she suggests I bring the DVD about John, share it with the staff, and talk about what happened. It's the last thing I want to do, but Donna quietly points out that my colleagues love me and respect me and have been grieving for John themselves with no way to express their feelings. She looks at me and says, "And this will be good for you as well."

When I get to the office, I ask Dorothy, my executive assistant, to send out an e-mail inviting any interested staff to come to the large conference room at one p.m. to meet with me and watch a video of John's life. I keep working in my office, dreading the meeting, wanting to bolt from the office, go home, and get under the covers. At 12:50 I walk down the hallway toward the large conference room, thinking about all the times in the last ten years I've walked down this hallway for a meeting in that room. Sometimes feeling anxious, sometimes being challenged, but usually excited, confident, grateful, in control, wanting to be here. Now I walk down the hallway feeling depressed, overwhelmed, traumatized, not in control, not wanting to be here.

Then I enter the conference room and I'm amazed. The room is crammed full of people. Some are sitting in chairs jammed around the long conference table, but most are standing, and people are spilling out both entrances. There are managers, program staff, support staff. Some of them are looking at me and some have their eyes lowered. As I walk through the door a woman nudges some people aside to make room for me. We're packed in there, shoulder to shoulder. I realize that these people are holding me up, figuratively and literally. I thank them for being here. I tell them that Donna said I had to do this for them and for me. I start to tell them what happened to John, but I can't continue because I'm crying. Someone turns out the lights and starts the DVD. I watch some of it but I'm more focused on being in the dark, crying more freely because no one can see me. But at the same time, I'm acutely aware of the love and support of all these friends and colleagues with whom I've worked for the last ten years.

The DVD ends and someone turns the lights on. I look around and see I'm not the only one crying. Some staff members quietly leave the conference room, hugging me as they walk out. One woman comes up to me, takes my hands, and says, "Every funeral should have a video. There should always be a celebration of life." Some of the staff members that I'm close to come up to me and we hold onto each other and cry. Dorothy gets the DVD out of the player and walks me back to my office. She hugs me, reflects on the outpouring of love and support I've just received, and says, "Donna was right about making you do this."

Part of me knows that Donna was right, and I'm glad that I've received the loving support of all these good people. But part of me still wants to retreat from the world, not share the DVD with anyone, not relive what happened, and not face the reality that my son is gone. I don't want to be the father of a dead son.

* * *

A day later I drive back down to John's place to pack his clothes. Among his tee shirts are some that his scuba diving group created. The group called themselves "The Bug Brothers" and they made tee shirts for each dive trip. Each member had a nickname. John's was "Shoot First." Those words are printed in script on the right front of each of John's shirts. I'm sure there's a story behind that. I fold the tee shirts and put them in a little pile. They're all different shades of blue and yellow. Printed on the front of each shirt is a small picture of a scuba diver capturing a lobster and stuffing it into his dive bag. On the back of the shirts is a picture of a large lobster stuffing a scuba diver into the lobster's dive bag. Eventually I'll give some of these shirts to a few family members and friends and I'll keep a couple for myself, but for now I'm holding onto them. I pack up John's other shirts and his suits, including the one he wore at my retirement dinner. I'll hold onto those too for a while.

I open the drawer where he kept all his jeans. I look at them and I fall apart. I remember that for most of the time John and I spent together throughout his entire life, we wore jeans: fishing, backpacking, sitting around the barbeque drinking beer. Before I know it I'm sitting on the floor next to his bed, holding four pairs of his jeans in my arms, crying and missing him more intensely than I have at any other time in this excruciating last month.

I drive home with his clothes, folded and placed in six cardboard boxes in the backseat. That night I watch the video of his life, something I will do often over the next six months, because by watching the video, I can stay connected with him in this life. Because no matter how much I hear his voice, no matter how much he is trying to tell me that he is in the next life, I can't let go. I want him back in this life.

* * *

The next day Donna and I have our first meeting with Janet Childs, a counselor and critical incident stress management trainer we've been referred to by SJPD. She's with the Center for Living with Dying in Santa Clara, near San Jose. Janet helps first responders deal with the emotional stress of the work they do. She's also been dealing with police and firefighter suicides for over thirty years, counseling family members who are survivors. As soon as we walk into her office her warmth and gentleness put us at ease. I'll see Janet for counseling and support on a regular basis for the next five years. She's loving and supportive and also a consummate professional, always helping me to climb out of my grief but always insisting that I don't take any shortcuts along the way.

We tell her about John and she lets us get through the whole pain-ful, tearful story. Then she gives us some preliminary advice. On the one hand the advice is obvious, but on the other hand it's crucial for our getting through these first few months: Janet tells us to be gentle with ourselves. She says we need to do that because we've been traumatized no differently than if we'd been severely injured physically. At first I don't understand, but she'll keep repeating this every time I see her in the coming months. I'll finally figure out that I'm supposed to stop beating myself up and start taking care of myself, and that doing so is not selfish.

Janet also tells us today to live in the moment, to take on one issue at a time, and to make no major decisions for awhile. She tells me I should determine what's hitting me the hardest at any particular moment and ad-dress that one issue. Finally she says that while we should try to have some structure in our life, we should allow for some down time and some nap time because the pain and grief will drain us of our physical energy. Now as I write this, six years after John's death, this is still true for me. Grief is exhausting.

Janet begins to tell us how things work with cops. The training and ori-entation of police officers prioritizes bringing control out of chaos, she says. When cops are confronted with a critical incident, they focus only on that situation, almost like going into a tunnel where everything is blocked out except their focus on the situation, the critical incident—and their need to decide how to respond. They are willing to risk everything during the criti-cal incident because they know the incident will come to an end. But when they become depressed in their personal lives—when they experience their own critical incidents—and can't control the situation causing the pain, they become deeply frustrated; they want closure and they can't get it. This leads them to feel like they're not functioning in any area of their lives and they feel ashamed. The highest-functioning individuals, the best cops, feel the deepest shame. And when they think the situation, or critical incident, will never end, they despair. They perceive themselves as a burden to all their loved ones, and they think that everyone will be better off if they're gone.

There is usually a triggering event that serves as the last straw. Then, for them, the only way to regain control is to decide to end their life. Once they decide to take control and end their life, even if they don't act upon the decision immediately, they appear to be calm because they *are* calm, because they feel relieved. They give no hint to those closest to them that they've decided to kill themselves. And they stop hearing external input— they are in the "tunnel."

For a few seconds, as I listen to Janet, I catch myself thinking that I can use this information to help John in his crisis. Then I'm back again in the horror and reality of John's suicide. Then I begin to see that this profile definitely applies to him in the last few months of his life. He told me that he didn't think he was functioning well at work, that he felt he was dragging down Alisa, that he was afraid he wasn't a good father to Kaitlin. I had told him that his perspective was clouded by his depression. I reminded him that Donna, a child development professional, told him more than once that he was doing a wonderful job with Kaitlin.

Sitting in Janet's office, I realize now that John couldn't hear any of what Donna and I said to him about all that. In mid-October he told me what a new and painful experience it was not to be able to control his situation; he also said he was having panic and anxiety attacks. In November he was served legal papers attempting to reopen the divorce, and this made him more distraught than ever. He had told me, "This will never end."

Somewhere in that period he made his decision, and he made sure I wouldn't know he'd made it. On the Saturday night a few days before he died, when we grilled lobsters on my back deck, he told me he was still depressed, but I noticed he was calm, without any signs of his earlier panic and anxiety. On Monday night, at my retirement dinner, he looked tired and I noticed that he had lost weight; but again, he appeared calm and acted pleased to be there, seeing my friends, feeling proud of his father. Janet thinks he may have put off acting on his decision because of my retirement dinner. She also thinks his decision produced the calmness I noticed.

As I write this, I know that I can't blame myself for not being aware of this profile of cops and suicide before John died, and I know that even if I had been aware of it, it might not have helped me stop him. But I wish I had known. I wish I had tried. I'm still overwhelmed by the fact that I wasn't able to see that my son, this lovely man, was in far greater pain than I could perceive. I was supposed to be his rock.

* * *

The day after our meeting with Janet, I drive down to meet Bruce and Alisa. I've asked them to take me to the place where John died. Donna isn't going. She says she doesn't want to see that place. She doesn't think I should go either, but I want to see and do anything that will connect me to John. I want to touch the ground where he had fallen. I want to be where he was at the end.

Bruce, Alisa, and I drive over to Henry Cowell State Park. It's a short trip. We park in the lot where John parked his truck. We walk up the trail,

Bruce in the lead. Bruce stops and tells me this is the spot. It's only sixty yards from the parking lot. A thick grove of trees separates us from the parking lot and the area is secluded, but I'm surprised that John didn't walk further into the forest. First I think that he wanted to make sure he'd be found, but then I remember that this entire trail is well used so he would have been found regardless of where he was. Then I begin to think of another possibility. Could he not wait any longer? Was he in so much pain he couldn't go farther?

Bruce and Alisa step away, and I stand on the spot where my son took his life, where his body lay on the ground all night, less than two months ago. I kneel down and touch the ground. I stand up and try to talk to him, but I can't. All I can do is stand there, asking myself how this happened. How did my son come to put a bullet through his temple? How did this beautiful boy come to such despair, such hopelessness? How did he end up dead on a mountain trail? How could I not see that he was in such pain that he could do this? I keep trying to talk to him, but I can't. I can only see him putting the gun to his head. I can only see his body lying on that trail all night. All I know is that he's gone, that I've lost him forever.

A few days later, on a Sunday afternoon, the phone rings. Donna's in the kitchen and picks it up. I'm at the dining room table going over some of John's real estate and bank files. Donna sticks her head into the dining room and with a look of puzzled amusement says, "It's Bruce and he has something to tell us, but he has to tell you first." I come into the kitchen; even though it's winter, sunlight is streaming through the kitchen window. I pick up the phone, plant myself on one of the stools around our island kitchen counter, and say hi to Bruce.

"Operation Deep Forest is successfully completed," Bruce says in his low, gravelly cop voice. I have no idea what he's talking about, but I already know, without hearing anything else, that this good man, my son's close friend and fellow scuba diver, has done something on behalf of John. Bruce reminds me of how much John loved the pine trees in the Sierras, and he tells me that John often mentioned that he and I were each other's rocks. So, Bruce goes on, he and Alisa and Steve Smith, another fellow cop and close friend of John's, bought a ten-gallon Ponderosa pine, snuck into Henry Cowell State Park, and planted the tree on the spot where John died. They also moved a large rock and placed it near the tree. "We damn near killed ourselves moving the boulder," Bruce says.

I picture the spot where John died and all of a sudden, unexpectedly, I'm back at the scene of his death, seeing my son's body on the trail, feeling the horror. Donna, standing by the sink, sees my reaction, and now she's concerned.

But then Bruce says, "We brought a bottle of Jameson and anointed the ground around John's memorial. And then we anointed ourselves. John got half and we drank the other half, with many toasts to John Francis Cahill." There's a pause and then Bruce says, "Okay, Brian, I have to confess."

"What do you have to confess?" I ask, completely puzzled.

"Actually, John only got a third of the Jameson and we got the rest," Bruce says in a sheepish tone of voice.

I laugh, and Donna relaxes. I thank Bruce and tell him how much I appreciate what they did. "John wasn't a big whiskey drinker so he wouldn't mind not getting much Jameson," I say. I hang up and tell Donna the whole story. We both laugh. It's not the first time I've cried since John took his life, but it's the first time I've laughed.

5

His Soul Never Touched the Ground

I HAVE MY SECOND session with Janet Childs in mid-January. As I sit in the waiting room I watch an elderly woman sitting there knitting, all her concentration on her knitting needles and her yarn. There's a middle-aged couple quietly talking. There's a woman in her mid-thirties who looks exhausted. My first thought is that this place feels like a dentist's office. Then it dawns on me that these people aren't here because they've lost a tooth. They're here because they've lost a loved one. Janet comes out to the waiting room, gives me a hug, and brings me into her office. As I sit on the small sofa across from her desk, I notice something I didn't notice the first time I was here, with Donna: there's a box of Kleenex on the coffee table in front of the sofa, one on the end table to my right, and a third box on Janet's desk. I used a lot of Kleenex the last time I was here. I'll continue to do so.

I review the activity of the last two weeks: the legal and financial issues, my packing John's things, my talking to John and beginning to hear him. I tell Janet that I'm beginning to experience bursts of panic; I'd felt some panic in the early stages of my divorce, but nothing like this. She tells me that panic attacks come from the shattering realization that the world is no longer safe, that anything can happen, that horror can happen, that the worst thing can happen, that the unbelievable can happen.

Then I bring up something that's been eating at me—my guilt about not calling John during the week before Thanksgiving, when I suspect now he was making the decision to kill himself. Janet points out that John told me not to hover, not to call him. He said, "If I need to talk to you I'll call," and he didn't call. She says he may have already made his decision by then; my call wouldn't have made a difference. By that point he probably couldn't see that the love of all of us would enable him to survive. He could only see his predicament. He thought everyone would be better off without him. He did it for others, not for himself. As for his last thoughts on the night he died, he was focused and linear—in a tunnel, Janet says. This was a manifestation of his training, but it was lethal because of his depression and despair. He was, at that point, not thinking of me, or anyone else. I sit there listening to Janet, remembering that on the night John shot himself, he may not have been thinking of me, but I was thinking of him—with a knot in my stomach, worrying about him, not realizing he was suicidal, not having a clue that he would be capable of suicide, and perhaps not allowing myself even to consider that possibility.

Some months later I will read *Night Falls Fast*, Kay Redfield Jamison's comprehensive exploration of suicide and her account of her own suicide attempt, "I did not consider it either a selfish or a not-selfish thing to have done. It was simply the end of what I could bear, the last afternoon of having to imagine waking up the next morning only to start all over again with a thick mind and black imaginings. No amount of love from others, and there was a lot, could help. I knew my life to be a shambles and I believed incontestably, that my family and friends and patients would be better off without me." I would come to realize that these words described what was going on in John. He had an abundance of love, a great job and a caring family, but that wasn't enough. He felt his life was a shambles and that everyone close to him would be better off if he was gone. But I hadn't read that book at that moment, when I was meeting with Janet, and even if I had I probably wouldn't have been able to fully take in what it said.

Sitting there with Janet I do suddenly remember that some years ago I read Andrew Solomon's book *The Noonday Demon: An Atlas of Depression*. Solomon writes from personal experience: "If you have never tried it yourself, you cannot begin to imagine how difficult it is to kill yourself." He adds, "An awful lot of people lead lives of quiet desperation and don't kill themselves because they cannot muster the wherewithal to do it."

I share this idea with Janet now. And through my tears I ask her: Was a life of quiet desperation the only alternative to suicide for my son? Why couldn't John hear me when I told him he would come out of this? Why couldn't the mantras that John wrote out give him a sense of hope? Why couldn't John understand that his role as a father was all-important? Why couldn't he be sustained by the love of all of us around him? She looks at me, hands me the Kleenex, and says, "Because it doesn't work that way."

Later I will read Thomas Joiner's book, *Myths about Suicide*. His major message is that when individuals become convinced that they are a burden and they do not belong, and their loved ones will be better without them, then the desire for death overcomes the urge for self-preservation. John got to that point. I don't know how, but he did. He was wrong, of course—absolutely no one was better off without him—but I believe that that was how he felt.

Joiner is clear that the suicidal mind is not primarily characterized by cowardice or anger: "My view is that those with no hesitation are the most fearless of all, people who have become fearless through either lengthy experience or mental preparation regarding their eventual means of death." Joiner adds, "Death by suicide requires staring the product of millions of years of evolution in the face and not blinking; it is tragic, fearsome, agonizing, and awful, but it is not easy. It is not the act of a coward." John Cahill—my son, Kaitlin's father, Krissy's father—was not a coward. He was wrong, but he was not a coward.

Joiner adds, "Some choose remote or anonymous locations of death, perhaps with the idea of buffering family from suicide's immediate aftermath." I believe that's why John went to Henry Cowell State Park in the Santa Cruz Mountains, and I also believe John was thinking of his family when he angled his weapon back so as not to disfigure his face.

I take some more Kleenex and then ask Janet about Donna and the pain she's feeling, not just because of John's death but also because of her pain in knowing how much I'm suffering. Janet says that it's good to honor how hard it is for Donna, but that I should not stop sharing with her how I'm feeling. A failure to share can cause real problems. "She has to be involved, and she's healthy enough to tell you when it is too much, and when it is too much you can stop and cry on each other's shoulders."

Donna and I will do a lot of crying on each other's shoulders in the coming years.

* * *

On the following Saturday Donna comes down to John's place with me. We finish packing most of John's possessions and Bruce comes by and helps us. Bruce and I each take a large carton down the stairs of John's condo and out to the parking lot. I put my carton down so I can open the trunk of Donna's car. Bruce places his carton in the trunk, and seeing that I'm still breathing hard, picks up my carton and puts it in the trunk. He closes the trunk, turns, and looks at me. Then he looks down and says, "John was the best man I ever knew." We stand in the parking lot, holding onto each other, missing John Cahill.

Later Donna and I take Krissy and Kaitlin to lunch at a local sandwich shop. The girls sit there, looking out the window, picking at their food and not talking. After lots of hugs and kisses, Donna and I drop them off at Michele's house and head home.

That night I have a long, intense panic attack. When it finally subsides, I realize that the experience isn't just a sudden burst of horror or a temporary sense of physical suffocation; it's an uncontrollable fear that the episode of panic will never end and that I'm powerless to end it. Is this what John was experiencing? Is this feeling what caused him to lose his way, what led him to hopelessness? Is this what led him up the trail?

* * *

I drive down to Scotts Valley on January 19 and do the final packing of John's things. Driving home that afternoon, I feel some of the pain and heaviness lightening up a bit. First I feel relief. Then I feel guilty. C. S. Lewis writes that along with the first signs of the lightening of grief "comes at once a sort of shame, and a feeling that one is under a sort of obligation to cherish and foment and prolong one's unhappiness." He thinks part of this is vanity. "We want to prove to ourselves that we are lovers on the grand scale, tragic heroes; not just ordinary privates in the huge army of the bereaved, slogging along and making the best of a bad job." The lightness for me will only last a few days, and I will soon return to the familiar territory of panic and pain. As I drive the twinge of guilt passes. I've begun to notice that the pain seems to come in surges; sometimes it's intense, at other times it recedes. Later I will read in George Bonanno's *The Other Side of Sadness*, "Grief is tolerable, actually, only because it comes and goes in a kind of oscillation."

The next day I sit at our dining room table opening the boxes I've just brought home from John's place. I go through all of John's 4-H awards, his stamp collection, high school yearbooks, newspaper accounts of his four years of varsity soccer, his college records, his police employment application, and the awards he garnered over the years. When I'm done I look at all the material spread over our dining room table, a bittersweet review of his whole life. But it wasn't a whole life. It was only half a life. There will be no memorabilia for what was supposed to be the second half of his life—no photos, no awards, no documentation, no memories, nothing. I box everything up to save it for Krissy and Kaitlin, along with John's police equipment and anything else that will be meaningful for his daughters. In the shower that night I hear, "Dad, I love you." I'm comforted, but all I can think of is that he's forty-two years old, and he is not supposed to be gone.

* * *

We had hired a probate attorney earlier to help us settle John's estate, but because Michele is attempting to reopen the divorce and involve me in that procedure, we also have to hire a family lawyer, Grey Cohen. Grey, a single father, reminds me that regardless of the specific conflict, Kaitlin is a minor and acting in her best interest and insuring in the long run that we have a close relationship with her should be our priority. I realized then and I still know now that he was right.

On January 21 Michele's petition to reopen the divorce is denied in court.

* * *

It's Inauguration Day. Barack Obama is making history. I don't care. I'm in the shower late that night, crying, missing John, wanting him back. I say to John, trying to believe it, "I know you're with God and with me."

I hear, "I am with God and with you, Dad."

I ask, "Then why do I miss you so much?"

I hear, "Because you're in the old life. You have to be in the new life, and then it won't hurt so much."

I ask, "What about Kaitlin?"

I hear, "I'm with her, but it may not show right away."

John's words, "You have to be in the new life," make me think about something Donna said early on, when John had only been dead for a few days. That night I woke up with a start in the middle of the night, seeing John's body on the trail out in the forest, in his tan jacket, blue jeans, and boots, lying there all night with a bullet through his head, alone. I was awake but the vision of John lying dead on that trail with no one to hold him was a nightmare. I started crying quietly, and then began trembling and sobbing loudly. Donna woke up and turned on the light and I told her what was going on. She looked me in the eye, hugged me hard, and said, "Remember! His soul never touched the ground! John went right to God."

Unknown to me at that time, and not surprisingly through the agency of my wife, God's grace began to work in me that night. It would be some time before I consciously experienced that unearned gift, that restoration of perspective, that sense of peace. But now, in the shower, hearing John refer to "the new life" reminds me of Donna saying John's soul never touched the ground. It also opens up the possibility in me that there's a way to think of my son not just in terms of losing him, not just in terms of his last, painful months of suffering, but in terms of the continuation of his spirit, his essence, his soul. I'm still too exhausted and depressed for any serious discernment, but hearing his voice, feeling that connection, hearing his reference to Kaitlin, gives me comfort.

* * *

The next day, Bruce calls and tells me he and a few other people have created a bumper sticker: "Never Forget John Cahill." He tells me they made two versions: one for sticking on cars and a smaller one for anything else you want to do with it.

The small version of that bumper sticker is still on the inside of my journal cover, on my laptop cover, and on the back of my Kindle. When I first heard about the sticker my initial response was that I didn't need a bumper sticker to help me remember John. But then I realized that maybe some folks would forget about him over time, and if a bumper sticker would help preserve his memory then I was all for it. I saw some of those stickers still on cars the last time I went to Scotts Valley, two years ago.

"Never Forget John Cahill." I don't have to worry about that happening to me. Sometimes, maybe a couple of times a week, I go a few minutes, even a few hours, without thinking about him. But forgetting—that's not within the realm of possibility.

* * *

On January 30, the St. Vincent de Paul truck comes by to pick up John's suits and six boxes of his clothes. I want them to be given to people who can use them, and I know John would approve, but as the driver pulls away I have to fight the urge to tell him to bring it all back. After the truck leaves, I close the garage door, sit on the floor in the dark, and cry.

That evening I'm grilling chicken on our back deck, and all of a sudden I realize it's my first time back here since I was drinking beer and grilling lobsters with John four days before he shot himself. I'm not sure I want to be here, on the deck or anywhere. In *Stations of the Heart*, Richard Lischer writes about the months after his son's death, "Grief is a series of caves—dark, multiple and unfathomed. You do not explore them. You fall into them. Which means you are constantly righting yourself and daily, sometimes hourly, recovering from little plunges into unrequited longing and despair."

That night I can't sleep. Around two thirty, I get in the shower and stay there until the hot water runs out, but it doesn't help. I get back into bed but I'm wide awake, wishing that I hadn't given away John's clothes, realizing that I don't want to go out on the deck again because John will never be there, because that's all I'll think about when I go out there. I'm lying there, wanting to hear his voice again, needing to hear his words, but there's nothing. He's gone.

I don't want to wake Donna so I get up, put on my robe, and go sit on the sofa in the living room in the dark. I think of what Janet told us about what happens to cops when they get depressed, and how for cops, because of their training and orientation, depression can lead to suicide. If I had known about this, could I have helped John? Could I have stopped him? I need to ask Janet. I need to know. It's five thirty and I can't call her now. But I need to see her today.

I call Janet at eight thirty. She can't talk but she says she can see me at eleven. I'm there at ten thirty. Today there's no one in the waiting room. Janet comes to get me, takes one look at me, and gives me a hug. We go into her office and she hands me a box of Kleenex. I'm crying, blowing my nose, and trying to get the question out. "If I had known about this profile of cops, depression and suicide, could I have stopped John from killing himself?"

Janet looks at me and says, "So that's what this is all about." She gets up, comes over, and sits next to me on the sofa. She starts to talk. I'm looking down and she gently takes my arm and says, "I want you to look at me." Then she tells me very clearly and firmly that from the point in time that John made up his mind, nothing could have changed the situation. No one, no matter how close or how loving, could have stopped him. She puts her arm on my shoulder and says, "Brian, you couldn't have stopped him. He wouldn't have let you." It will take me a long time to accept that. I'm his father. He died on my watch.

Janet and I review the last few weeks before John died, especially my feelings about all the things I didn't see or do, and the week before Thanksgiving when I didn't call John. I'm burning through a lot of her Kleenex. She tells me that the more I can flesh out the details, the better off I will be. I'm just beginning to get a hint of the value of doing this, but it's so tempting to deny the details. If I can ignore the details, not focus on them, not allow myself to go back over everything that happened to my son and to me, then maybe it won't hurt so much. And some days I just want it to not hurt. I know I can't undo what happened to John, but my motive here is the same reason I stay under the covers some mornings or stay in the shower at midnight until the hot water runs out. It's a way to escape. And some days I just want to escape. But most days I know I can't.

Janet tells me that John's presence at my retirement dinner and his bringing lunch to Alisa on the last day were elaborate, genuine expressions of love, and at the same time there was just too much pain for John to continue and, he thought, too much pain for all of us. She tells me it's acceptable to be angry, brokenhearted and understanding—accepting his new life and loving him—all at the same time. I've been waiting to feel anger about what he did, anger at him for leaving his daughters, for leaving me, but it hasn't happened. I also tell Janet more about hearing John talk to me while I'm in the shower and other places. She agrees that it's good to focus on John in his new life, but she cautions me that I still have a lot to process about how he ended his old life.

Before I leave her office, she says, "There's one more thing I need to tell you today." She explains that sometime in the next few months the shock of what happened will begin to wear off and only then will I begin to feel the real horror, pain, and loss of John's death. The shock serves as a filter to protect us from being overwhelmed when there's a catastrophe. I look at her and say, "I don't see how it can get any worse."

She takes my hands and says quietly, "It will." I leave, not understanding what she is trying to tell me.

That night I have a panic attack. I'm overwhelmed by the reality that my son, my strong, healthy boy—my rock—put a bullet through his head. And I'm flooded with shame that I didn't protect him. Maybe this is what Janet meant by the filter wearing off.

In early February we fly to east to Pittsburgh to spend time with Donna's family. On the plane I realize that I have no interest in the plans I made for my retirement. I'd intended to join a couple of nonprofit boards and work at the UC School of Social Welfare in a new leadership program for nonprofit executives. But now I have no interest or energy for any of that. I know I want to eventually get back to volunteering at San Quentin prison, something I've been doing for the last three years. Because of John's loss I feel more connected to the guys there. I don't know their specific experiences and they don't know mine, but even though they're inside and I'm outside we share the common ground of pain and loss. I know I'll be spending a lot of time on John's affairs and I want to be present for Krissy and for Kaitlin. I'm also beginning to have a vague notion that I might work in suicide prevention for cops.

The days in Pittsburgh are restful. Donna's parents and her sisters' families are low-key and quiet and I feel their love and support. Then, a couple of nights into the visit, I have another panic attack. I'm lying in bed in Donna's old bedroom, unable to sleep, realizing that I appreciate this large family but somewhere down deep, I resent the fact that all their children are alive.

A few nights after we get home from Pittsburgh, I'm lying in bed, again wide-awake. I'm getting used to the panic and horror, realizing more clearly than ever the finality of what happened, but I'm also buried in guilt and shame that I let John slip through my fingers.

The next night Donna reads night prayers and Psalm 31: ". . . In you O Lord I take refuge, you are my rock and my stronghold." John was my rock, and I'm still not ready to see God as my rock.

Two days later, awake at four a.m., I say to John, "I miss you so much."

I hear, "I know. You have to stay in the new life and then it won't hurt so much." John knows I'm a slow learner. These are the same words I heard a few weeks ago. But now, unlike then, I soak up the phrase "the new life" and realize more fully what he's trying to tell me. I haven't lost him. I can still be connected to him. He's gone from this life, but he's still around.

But I also realize that he's warning me. If I can't hold on to this thought, this way of seeing him, it's going to hurt. If I slip back into thinking only of him in his old life, it's going to hurt. And I know he's right.

* * *

Later in February Donna and I are in Scotts Valley meeting with Michele and seeing the girls. Kaitlin doesn't try to hide her pain at missing her dad and her confusion over what happened. She talks quietly with Donna. I'm devastated to see her this way, but Donna reminds me later that it's important for Kaitlin to express what she's feeling.

That night Donna and I go a movie. Donna goes to get the popcorn. Sitting there in the dark before the show starts, I say to John, "I'm okay because of Donna, because you're talking to me, and because I know you're with Kaitlin."

I hear, "I'll continue to talk to you, I am with Kaitlin, and you're right about Donna."

I can see him smiling, and again I'm beginning to grasp that John is in his new life. I sit there in the dark theater knowing that John's spirit is alive. I'm connected to him. I haven't lost him. I can still see him smiling. And I smile too.

When Donna comes back with the popcorn, I tell her what I heard and what I'm thinking. She grabs my hand, smiles, and whispers, "Wow! See?"

I sit there, completely oblivious to the movie, not hogging the popcorn the way I usually do. And in that moment, because now I can grasp the concept of John's new life, I begin to think of him as being with God. I still can't climb that metaphysical hill, but I realize that if John's spirit is living, and if God exists, then somehow John is in God's presence. He is "with God." I will wrestle more with all of this, but right now I'm comforted.

The next day we join John's close friends in a celebration of thanksgiving for John's life. Bruce and John Weiss tell me how much John talked about me, recounting our outdoor adventures and misadventures and making it clear how proud of me he was. I love being with John's friends, and I'm desperate for any connection to John, but at the same time it's painful to be here. I'm slow to realize how painful it is, but Donna knows. She'd realized when we were invited to this gathering that it would be painful and tried to tell me then, but I couldn't hear it. But now, standing in Bruce's living room, I'm feeling exactly what Donna was afraid I would feel. John is gone. His friends are expressing their love and respect for him in his absence—his permanent, irreversible absence. My desire to be connected to John through his friends is swallowed up by the undeniable reality of his death. We are only here because of his death, because he is gone.

When we get home, I open the mail and get the renewal bill for John's long term care insurance, and also a notice for him to serve on jury duty. I've sent notices to all the appropriate places, but obviously not everyone has paid attention. After Mass one morning at our parish, someone who didn't know about John's death asks me how I was enjoying my retirement. They obviously didn't get the notice.

6

Dad, I'm Okay

I'M HAVING DISBELIEF ATTACKS—ACTUALLY going for a second or two thinking John is still alive, and then realizing that he's gone and feeling the crunch of the horror again. This will happen on a regular basis over the next few months. And I still wake up in the morning once in a while and exist for a few seconds before I remember that John is gone. Mary Allen, in *The Rooms of Heaven*, writes, "Every morning when I woke up there'd be a tiny window of time when I'd feel good before I remembered he was dead."

Now, in the middle of March, I'm overwhelmed with my own depression and with handling John's affairs, including opening probate and dealing with his pension and the various conflicts with Michele. I'm beginning to realize that what Janet was trying to tell me would happen, is happening: the initial shock is wearing off; it's no longer serving as a filter for the real horror and pain of John's suicide. Iris Bolton says it best: "The pain remained, lodged in my entrails like a fishhook."

I'm trying to hold onto my newfound view that John is in his new life, in his spirit life. But my new perspective has little foundation to support it, and it's easily washed away by the still-fresh horror of what happened to my son, the still-raw pain of his loss, and my desire to be connected with him in his old life, the way I knew him, to have him in my life.

I drive to Scotts Valley to meet with our other attorney, Dale Dawson, on the probate issues. Later I stop by the site of John's death. I sit by the tree and the rock that John's friends brought here. After about ten minutes I hear, "Dad, I'm okay."

I answer, "I'm not always okay."

I hear, "You will be."

I'll come to realize that he's right—I will be okay. But I'm still a slow learner, and at this moment, standing where my son ended his life, I'm not so sure I'll be okay. And I'm not sure I want to come back here.

* * *

March is far more painful than February, not just because the shock is fading away and the pain is so intense, but because I have so many disbelief attacks, followed each time by the crushing realization that John is undeniably and permanently gone from my life. I try to focus on his new life and my new relationship with him, but the pain burns, and life is upside down. In the aftermath of his daughter's death, Roger Rosenblatt writes, "We will never feel right again."

During the last week in March, a parole violator kills four Oakland police officers. I have some idea what their families are going through, and I try to pray for them. In the shower that night I say to John, "I miss you and it hurts."

I hear, "I know, but it won't always hurt this much." I am glad I don't know it then, but this will be the last time I'll hear John speak to me.

* * *

Roger Rosenblatt writes about sensing his daughter's presence: "I felt a hand touch my right wrist, not softly, so that it might be mistaken for a flutter or a breeze on my sleeve, but definite, like a comforting pat one person might give another." And then he adds, "I hoped to feel that touch again, but I did not. And I have not felt it since." In the end Rosenblatt questions whether what he felt came from his daughter. "It might have been a small spasm, an involuntary movement of my forearm. Something like a twitch."

I know that hearing John's voice was not a twitch. I know that when I heard him in the shower a week after the funeral, when he told me we were connected—that was not a twitch. And a month after that, when I heard him tell me that he was with God and not in pain, and then about a month later, when he told me to see him in his new life—these were not twitches. The words, the phrases he used, the tone of his voice—they were *John*.

* * *

I still haven't absolved myself of responsibility for John's death, but I keep thinking about what Janet told me about cops, depression, and suicide. I'm getting a better understanding of John's frustration, anger, and pain, and even his shame, but I'm still struggling to understand how his love for Kaitlin and Krissy, and for all his loved ones, and our love for him, could not sustain him. I call Janet, but she can't see me for a few days because she's helping the Oakland Police Department deal with the loss of their officers.

When I meet with her she gently points out that John's thinking was flawed, that he loved Kaitlin and Krissy but didn't think he'd be able to show that love over time, and he thought that he wouldn't be allowed to have a real father/daughter relationship with them. He also felt that all those close to him would be better off if he died, and he knew that because of Donna I would survive.

Kay Redfield Jamison reminds those of us who are survivors that we'll never completely understand: "Suicide will have seemed to its perpetrator the last and best of bad possibilities, and any attempt by the living to chart this final terrain of life can be only be a sketch, maddeningly incomplete." I'm coming to understand more about John's last few months. I'm coming to understand how cops are susceptible to suicide. But I'll never have a complete picture. And it will always be maddening.

Some of my confusion arises from retracing the last three days of John's life. He was at my retirement dinner and clearly enjoyed watching his father being honored, being with Donna, and seeing my friends. On Tuesday, when he took Kaitlin to the therapist, he showed no signs of suicidal thinking or behavior, and he was talking positively about the future. While the officers who were his close friends were aware of his depression and devastation, none of them saw specific indicators of suicidal behavior on Wednesday, John's last day on this earth. Alisa didn't see any signs when he brought her lunch that day.

Thomas Joiner explains some of this. Based on the research, he believes that those who die by suicide experience two thought processes at the same time, one relating to mundane daily plans and activities, the other relating to the comfort they take in the thought of ending their life. "Though it is difficult and uncomfortable to conceive of this last process, it does not change the fact that it is a true process that characterizes the minds of suicidal people. It is even more difficult to come to terms with the fact that people can harbor this very unusual state of mind at exactly at the same time they are thinking of weekend plans, or mowing the lawn, or going to the grocery store."

I also tell Janet about continuing to hear John's voice. She suggests that because I'm so consciously aware of not imagining or conjuring up these experiences, they're probably authentic. I think they are authentic. I want them to be authentic. I need them to be authentic. If they're not authentic, then every part of John is gone. His spirit is gone. If they're not authentic, then I'm gone.

Before I leave Janet's office, she reminds me again that I did nothing wrong, but she acknowledges that even at forty-two John was my child and the feeling of him "slipping through my fingers" is valid in that I was helpless to stop this from happening. She cautions me that I'll be experiencing intense pain and feelings of vulnerability for the next few months. She's right. March 30 is John's forty-third birthday.

* * *

One day during this time I'm in my study finally facing a task I've been putting off: organizing all the materials from John's funeral. I'm looking at a picture of John in his San Jose Police uniform, the picture that was at the back of the church during the funeral Mass. I glanced at it as I walked past it on the morning of the funeral, but I didn't really see it. At that moment in time I wasn't concentrating on anything except trying to breathe, trying not to crumble, trying to hold onto Donna. I look at the picture now. It's a blow-up and John is wearing his dress blue uniform. His hat hides his closely cropped brown hair and receding hairline. The slight cleft in his chin is visible; he inherited that from Karen's father, Fritz. He has his bushy brown cop's mustache and his typical John sweet smile. Today as I look at the picture I really notice the smile. In all of John's other police pictures, especially the motors pictures, he has this cop look of confidence, competence, and authority—not a scowl, but definitely not the sweet smile that I know so well. The sweet smile that so comforted me, the smile of his childhood and teen years, the smile he wore when we shared a beer or ended a day of backpacking, the smile he had when he talked about Krissy and Kaitlin, the sweet smile that I thought would always be there.

I look back at the picture. I don't know yet what I'm going to do with it. Probably I'll give it to Kaitlin. But right now, this morning, I just want to have it in my presence, to be able to look at my son, to see his sweet smile, to feel how glad I am that this picture shows his tender side, shows him, even in his uniform and badge, as he's always been loving, loveable—my beautiful boy.

* * *

It's a Thursday afternoon in early April and I'm at my desk, having spent most of the day on John's paperwork. I need to get out of the house. I drive over to Land's End and park my car near the head of the Golden Gate

Coastal Trail. I've been out here many times with Donna and a few times with John. I remember when my first marriage was ending and I walked out here, depressed about my divorce and uncertain about my future. I always thought that day would be my lowest point on this trail. Now, as I start walking, I would gladly trade that day in the fall of 1996 for this day in the spring of 2009, four months after my son's death.

It's a cool, overcast day with low, heavy fog. I look to my right. The towers of the Golden Gate Bridge are barely visible. I look down at the gray-green water. This is the water where we distributed my dad's ashes in 1995. I sit on a bench and zip up my parka. I think of my dad and realize that after his death I missed him, but I never questioned my belief that his soul lived on. Then I think of John and how I've heard his voice a number of times, reminding me that we are still connected, that he is with God and he is in his new life.

* * *

As I sit there, I think of a book I read when I was in Pittsburgh with Donna's family, a novel called *The Shack*. It's about a father whose daughter was abducted and murdered, and the major themes are God's love, free will, and the existence of evil. At this time in my life, four months after John's suicide, I'm not clear about God's love, though I'm certainly clear about the existence of evil in the world. I get the idea that free will allows us to choose between good and evil, between love and hate, but it's always been just a concept for me. Nowadays I have a stark, raw realization of what can follow from free will. And now, in light of the choice my son made, I have a better appreciation of why Dostoyevsky's Grand Inquisitor, in *The Brothers Karamazov*, condemned God for endowing humans with the burden of free will. And I wonder if God realized the amount of pain and suffering, chaos and destruction He was unleashing when He gave us free will. Why, I wonder, couldn't He have set some limits, given us free will in everything except the capacity for genocide and suicide?

I hike back on the trail toward my car. I can't see the bridge towers at all. I can't see the water. Everything is covered in fog. Everything is dark.

* * *

A few days later I check my e-mail and see a message from Michele. Even before I open the e-mail, there's a knot in my stomach.

In the e-mail Michele says that because her effort to reopen the divorce and sue for a portion of John's estate has been rejected in court, she's requesting a substantial portion of John's estate—a sum she says will allow her to keep the house and continue to make the payments. The e-mail details the amounts she wants and for what purposes.

I sit there looking at the computer screen, remembering how angry I felt when I received notice of Michele's lawsuit just two weeks after John's funeral. Now, rather than waste time and energy on anger, I compose a detailed response to Michele's itemized request. I remind her that when John asked her to sign off on a short sale of the house she refused. I remind her that my role is to use the proceeds of John's estate for the education and future of his daughters. I offer her an amount that I believe represents John's obligations during the last months before his death. I let my draft e-mail sit for a few days to make sure I'm not writing out of anger, or at least to make sure the anger doesn't spill out into my message, and then I send it off.

Each morning for the next three days, I hesitantly check my e-mail. On the fourth day, Michele responds, clearly upset, dismissing my offer, threatening further legal action, telling me that I only knew John's side of the story, and declaring that she doesn't want to have anything to do with us. In April there are further e-mails back and forth, some from Donna trying to work out a time for us to see Kaitlin, some from Michele expressing more anger, and some from me, doing a bad job of hiding my anger. During that time we have dinner with Krissy a couple of times. She's moved into her own apartment—she's twenty and ready to be on her own—and she's trying to stay out of the conflict between her mom and us. But eventually she'll let us know that she is hurting, she is missing her dad, and she is angry at how we are responding to her mom. I get another e-mail from Michele in April. In the e-mail she makes it clear that she's not going to let us have any contact with Kaitlin.

I print out the e-mail and show it to Donna at the end of the day when she gets home from work. Then we sit at the kitchen counter and look at each other, and I can see in her eyes that she feels the same way I do: this is a nightmare on top of a nightmare. Not having contact with Kaitlin is unthinkable. And Donna points out how unthinkable it is for Kaitlin too—to have lost her dad and now to lose us. We don't know it at the time, but we won't see our granddaughter for two years—until March 2011.

As I write this now, I realize I didn't understand how traumatized Michele was by John's suicide, how protective she was of her girls, how frightened she was about her financial situation, and how hurt she was by the blame and criticism she received for her role in what happened. But in the spring of 2009, all I could feel was anger and despair. All I could feel was that my son was gone and, for the foreseeable future, so was my granddaughter.

Jamison writes, "Death by suicide is not a gentle deathbed gathering; it rips apart lives and beliefs, and it sets its survivors on a prolonged and devastating journey."

We are ripped apart and on a devastating journey.

* * *

One morning in early April I bring a large packet of mail up to the dining room and sit down to sort it out. There are bills, magazines, subscription offers, and the usual junk mail. At the bottom of the pile is an oversized, battered brown envelope. I start to toss it in the junk pile, assuming it's some low-budget marketing material. Then I notice that it's addressed to me, the address is hand-printed, and I see that the return address is San Quentin State Prison, again hand-printed. I'm puzzled, because this is clearly not any kind of official document and none of the inmates at San Quentin would have my address.

I open the beat-up envelope. Inside is an eight-by-eleven-inch handmade card. The front of the card has a hand-painted picture of a blue-and-white dove surrounded by a green wreath with red and yellow roses in it. My name is printed above the wreath and below it says, "With our deepest regrets." Inside the card are thirty signatures of San Quentin inmates. Father Steven Barber, the Catholic Chaplain at San Quentin, has also signed the card. Now I realize how this card got to me: Father Barber sent it. I haven't been back to the prison where I have volunteered for three and a half years since John's death four months ago.

I sit at the dining room table reading each individual note on the card, crying and trying not to get tears on the card. All of a sudden I'm reminded that in a world of suffering and chaos there's still love, and sometimes that love comes from unlikely sources. How often does the family of a cop who died receive a condolence card from a bunch of lifers in a state prison? After I stop crying, I write a thank-you note to the guys and send it to Father Barber.

I haven't returned to San Quentin since John died because I feel like I don't have the energy to worry about other people's problems. But a week after I get the card, I realize that even though I still don't have a lot of energy, I want to go over to the prison for Sunday Mass—to personally thank the men for their card, but also because John's death has made me feel even closer to them. While their suffering is different from mine, now I can truly relate to them, because now I truly understand what suffering is.

* * *

On the following Sunday morning, I drive over the Golden Gate Bridge and head north on 101. As I come through Corte Madera and look east, I see the massive, tan, fortress-like cellblocks of San Quentin. And I think of how, as I have every time I've seen this view since I started volunteering at the prison, I used to glance over at this place in the days before I started going there with no thought for the individuals confined inside it, no thought about whether all of them deserved to be there or whether any of them had developed insight into themselves and remorse for their crimes.

Today as I enter the prison I feel a little anxious, but it's not the anxiety I felt when I first started coming into this grim environment. My anxiety today comes from knowing that once again I'm going to be on the wrong end of expressions of sympathy. I sign in at the east gate, pick up my volunteer identity card, walk up to the main sally port, sign in again, and eventually get to the main courtyard of the prison.

The Catholic chapel is on my right. When I enter the vestibule Father Barber comes over immediately and greets me. He's a young, dedicated Jesuit with close-cropped dark-red hair and intense blue eyes. He gives me a warm hug and tells me that today's Mass is being offered in memory of John Cahill. I thank him and ask him if the guys have read my thank-you note for their card. He points to the bulletin board next to his office where my note is hanging. "They've all read it," he says. Then he looks at me and says, "I think it would be good for them and for you if you thanked them directly."

Even though I've come here to thank the men in person, I grimace now and say, "I know. But I'm not exactly comfortable doing that." I can't get past feeling uncomfortable being on the receiving end of sympathy—I'm good at giving it, I guess, but not good at getting it. I never knew that about myself until now, and I feel a little surprised to be learning something new about myself in the midst of everything that's going on.

Father Barber seems to know what I'm feeling without me having to spell it out. He smiles and says, "You'll be fine."

I'm not so sure.

I leave the vestibule and enter the chapel. Coming toward me down the main aisle is my friend Lorenzo, followed by some other inmates. Lorenzo is the leader of the restorative justice group. He's a stocky forty-two-year-old Hispanic who's in for second-degree murder. Even though he struggled with alcohol during high school, he won a partial university scholarship and was going to be the first person in his family to go to college. Four days before he was supposed to start school his father told him there wasn't enough money for him to begin his first semester. Then he learned that his girlfriend wanted to end their relationship. He was hurt, angry, and depressed. He took his father's pistol and went to a nearby park.

He considered suicide but instead decided to go to the local high school and try to convince his girlfriend not to break up with him. He took the bullets out of the pistol that would fire the next few times he pulled the trigger, thinking he would scare his girlfriend by pointing the gun at her and pulling the trigger on an empty chamber. He confronted his girlfriend and they argued; she tried to walk away; he took out the pistol, pointed it at her chest, and pulled the trigger. It turned out the gun's barrel rotated counter-clockwise instead of clockwise as most revolvers do, and the hammer hit a live round. When the police arrived they found Lorenzo cradling the dying girl in his arms. At eighteen Lorenzo was convicted of second-degree murder and sentenced to fifteen years to life. The judge told him that if he behaved himself he would be out in twelve years. He's been behind bars for twenty-three.

Over that time has demonstrated deep insight and remorse for his crime. He's also educated himself, becoming skilled in computerized sheet metal fabrication, and taken a series of courses in something called the School of Pastoral Leadership, a Catholic adult education program. Lorenzo organized the Catholic adult education program within San Quentin, gathering about a dozen other inmates who wanted to take classes and arranging for instructors to come to the prison. The courses cover Catholic teaching and values, liturgy and worship, evangelization and leadership development. Lorenzo regularly attends Mass, has a serious prayer life, and is the most spiritually mature man I've met in this place.

He comes up to me now and hugs me so hard he almost squeezes the breath out of my chest. He holds on and whispers in my ear, "I'm glad you're back."

My eyes fill up and all I can say is, "Me too."

We don't know it at the time, but Lorenzo will be released in a year, go on to graduate from college with a degree in business, and become an advocate for reentry services for paroled inmates.

Then Ron, an older, white-haired man, comes up to me and shakes my hand. Ron is serving twenty-one years to life for second-degree murder. He tells me that he's been praying for me and for John's daughters every day. Then Dwayne, a fifty-year-old African-American convicted of armed robbery and murder, puts his arm around my shoulder and tells me that his mother has been praying for me. Dwayne will be released in two years and take a job working with delinquent youth, trying to talk them out of the gang life. More of the guys greet me and embrace me. Then Father Barber, led by his inmate altar servers, their white albs covering their blue prison dungarees, walks up the main aisle to the altar and begins Mass. I take a seat next to Ron, completely forgetting that I didn't want to be on the receiving end of sympathy.

After Mass, Father Barber says to the men, "Many of you know Brian Cahill. He has been coming in here for the last three and a half years. He has something he wants to say to you." I stand up, walk up to the altar, and look out at 250 men. They're all different ages, different races, different levels of faith, but they're all dressed in blue shirts and blue jeans. I catch my breath and say, "After my son died, we received over two hundred condolence cards and letters. They were all appreciated. But the most meaningful condolence message came from here, from this chapel, from thirty of you guys. I don't know if it's unique, but it's pretty special that the family of a cop who dies would receive a condolence message from a bunch of San Quentin prisoners."

The men smile at that and I'm planning to say thanks and get off the altar. But then it comes to me that I want—need—to tell them about John, not about how he died but about how he lived, what kind of a cop he was. "My son was a police officer for nineteen years," I say. "Any of you who are from San Jose might have had some contact with him. John Cahill loved being a cop. But I want you to know, not just from my observations, but also from checking his record, that he never lost his humanity out there. He was never a racist. He was never disrespectful to those he encountered on the street." I pause, and I see a number of men nodding thoughtfully, appreciatively. I see others, guys I know, looking at each other and smiling, almost as if they're saying, "Well, that's not surprising."

I thank the men again for the card and for their love and support. They give John and me a standing ovation. As I walk back to my pew I start to weep. I think about how crying usually isn't a good thing to do in front of a bunch of prisoners. I wish I wasn't crying, even though I know these men aren't what you think of normally when you think of a bunch of prisoners. But then I notice that some of the men in the pews are fighting back their own tears. I sit down and Ron puts his arm around me. "Your pride in your son is so clear," he whispers to me. I look at him but I don't say anything. I can't.

I look at the men sitting in the pews around us. I see a young man in brand-new prison-issue dungarees. He can't be more than twenty. I see a tiny, old, frail, Hispanic man who, I will learn later, has been in prison for over fifty years. I see old, young, black, white, Hispanic, and Asian men; men with shaved heads and others with ponytails.

All of these men, including Ron, have done horrendous things and caused horrendous suffering. And they've suffered themselves, in their punishment, in their regret and remorse and in their realization of the suffering they've caused others. I know that most of the world writes them off as los-ers, destroyers, with no redeeming value, but as I look around the chapel I feel nothing but love and gratitude for their support and empathy. They've suffered in different ways than I have, ways I can't really know, but we've all suffered mightily nonetheless, and in our suffering, theirs and mine, there's a common bond. God's grace flows through these men. I can feel it almost palpably here, now, in this chapel. And I realize that today, here—in San Quentin Prison—I'm a recipient of that grace, and these men are my brothers.

7

Ride Along

IT's A SATURDAY MORNING in April 2009 and I'm at my desk, putting all of John's records—his documents that we've brought to our house so I can go through them—in a cardboard file box. Most of the material relates to pension, insurance, banking, real estate, health coverage, and his police documents. I notice one file labeled "miscellaneous," which I don't remember seeing before. I open the file and there are some boot catalogues, some brochures from central coast wineries, a DVD, and a nine-by-twelve-inch brown envelope. I open the envelope and glance at what's inside. I see that it's a collection of cartoons depicting John Cahill, penned by his dear friend John Weiss.

I had found one of these cartoons in John's books when I was packing his things in January. Now I hold the envelope, torn between wanting to look at the cartoons, wanting to have another way to be connected to my son, and at the same time wanting to mail the cartoons back to John Weiss without looking at them. I'm tempted to do the latter to avoid the pain I know I'll feel if I look at the cartoons, to avoid another reminder that my son is gone. But I quickly realize I have to see them. I start to cry before I even pull the first one out.

It's a drawing of an eager young Officer Cahill trying to catch unsuspecting speeders on Highway 17 in Scotts Valley. The cartoon shows John crouching on top of a speeding SUV, desperately trying not to fall off and excitedly calling for backup on his radio. The caption below the cartoon reads: "Cahill bucking for officer of the month." The next cartoon captures John on a white water rafting trip, holding a bottle of wine and a full glass while at the same time trying to keep an entire case of wine from falling out of the raft. There's one of an unshaven, overweight, disheveled Officer Cahill, sitting in a SJPD patrol car, welcoming another transfer from Scotts

Valley PD, telling him how great it is to work in San Jose. There's one that re-calls a real-life incident in Scotts Valley, where John inadvertently rolled his patrol car over the foot of an elderly woman—the cartoon shows the woman getting her revenge by backing her car over John and his motorcycle.

I spread all the cartoons out on my desk. I'm crying but I'm also smil-ing, enjoying these clever, hilarious and not-always-flattering portrayals of John Cahill. I sit there, so aware that he's gone and yet also so aware that until he lost his way he lived a full, rich, vibrant life and he was blessed with friends—friends like John Weiss who could love him fiercely and at the same time poke fun at him.

Then I pick up the DVD that was in the envelope with the cartoons. It's labeled "Real Stories of the Highway Patrol." *Real Stories of the Highway Patrol* was a half-hour syndicated television series that ran from 1993 to 1999, featuring reenactments of actual Highway Patrol cases. I remember John telling me he appeared in one episode, about a case he was actually involved in. He told me that he'd played a minor role in the case and didn't make a big deal out of being on the program. At the time it didn't seem like that big a deal to me either, and I never watched the show, but now I can't wait to watch it—to see John alive, doing his job, moving through the world.

I take the DVD upstairs and put it into the DVD player. Donna, my unofficial technical assistant, isn't home, and it takes me a while to get ev-erything working right. Then I do, and as I sit there getting ready to push the play button, I realize that just like the cartoons, this is going to hurt. But I want to see John. No matter how much pain is involved, I will always want to see John.

I watch the first part of the show, waiting for John to turn up on the screen. There are scenes of a stocky, middle-aged guy with dark glasses com-ing into a convenience store. He suddenly reaches over the counter, shoves a gun in the clerk's face, and forces the clerk to open the cash register. The gunman grabs all the cash and rushes out of the store. In the next set of scenes, the same man comes up behind a woman in an East Bay parking lot. The woman has a bag of groceries in her hand, and she's opening the door of her blue-and-white pickup truck. The man grabs her, shoves her into the truck, gets in next to her, pulls out a knife, and demands the keys to the truck. Then he throws her out of the truck and takes off.

That's when John shows up on the screen, sitting in his patrol car parked near a gas station adjacent to a Highway 17 on-ramp. It's evening, but the lighting is good. It's a profile shot of his face and head, and I can see him clearly. He looks so strong and healthy with his tanned face and his bushy cop's mustache. He spots the blue-and-white pickup pulling into the gas sta-tion, then suddenly turning around and driving off in the other direction.

John calls in the description and license plate number, his voice firm and professional. The dispatcher tells him the truck is reported as stolen.

The scene changes and now John is following the truck as it heads south on a road that parallels the highway. John follows and turns on his lights and siren. The truck speeds up with John in full pursuit. He calls in the description and location of the truck and the direction it's heading. As the truck leaves Scotts Valley and races toward Santa Cruz, two highway patrol cars soon take over the chase, and the rest of the program is about the highway patrol officers capturing the felon.

I turn off the DVD, realizing that John played down his appearance on the show because he only appeared in two brief scenes. But I loved seeing him. I loved seeing him at work. I sit there thinking about how much he loved his work. I know he was proud of what he did, proud to be a police officer. Even though he played down his role in this episode, I think he was secretly pleased to be on TV.

When he was at Scotts Valley I did two ride-alongs with him. Most police departments allow for ride-alongs as a way to educate citizens and engender support for law enforcement. I'd done a number of ride-alongs in San Francisco with various cops when I was working with delinquent youth. The first time I rode with John he was at the end of his first year of working in Scotts Valley. The ride-along was an uneventful three hours, but that didn't matter to me because I was sitting next to my son, Officer John Cahill. I remember repeatedly glancing over at him, watching him in his still-new uniform, me bursting with pride, respecting the career choice he made. A few years later I did another ride-along with him.

Here's how I remember that one: It's a late weeknight evening and John is patrolling north on the part of Highway 17 that runs through Scotts Valley. A pickup truck passes us on the right, and John notices that the man is driving without a seatbelt. John moves in behind the truck, flashes his red light, and the truck pulls over onto the shoulder of the road. John gets out of the patrol car, telling me to stay where I am in the front passenger seat. I watch my son approach the driver from the left rear side of the driver's truck. John's right hand is resting lightly on his holstered weapon. He takes the man's license and comes back to the patrol car to run a check on the driver.

When John returns to the truck he asks the man if he's been drinking, and the man answers that he drank two beers in the last hour. John has him step out of his car and begins to administer a series of tests on the man to determine if this is a DUI situation. The man has difficulty following John's directions and keeps interrupting John, saying he just wants to go on his way. The man is slightly belligerent, suggesting, at least from my point of view, the possibility of violence. At one point the guy complains that the shoulder of the road isn't level. John responds patiently and calmly, "That's a good point. Let's move up to this level piece of ground where it should be easier for you." A bit later, when the man is midway through one of the dexterity tests John is administering, the man drops his hands and says impatiently, "Look, just let me go." John says, more firmly now, "Sir, I'm not going to let you go until I know that it's safe for you to drive. So if you want to get through this, you need to cooperate." Finally John tells the man that he has to take the Breathalyzer test. The man backs up and says, "I don't want to. I just want to get out of here."

John, all business now, gets right in front of the guy and says, "You can refuse the test and then I'll be required to arrest you. You can take the test and flunk and I will arrest you. Or you can take the test and if you pass you can go on your way. So the only way for you to go on your way is to take the test." The man sullenly agrees. John administers the Breathalyzer, and the man's alcohol level is well over the limit. John arrests him, cuffs him, places him in the back seat, and we transport him back to the Scotts Valley PD.

That night it was obvious to me that not only did John love this work, he was doing exactly what he wanted to do and what he was good at. I continued to feel the truth of that over the next few years after John transferred to San Jose. I knew police work involved some danger, but I felt that John was well-trained and had the right mindset to be a good cop. He had no need to be overly aggressive, yet at the same time he was capable of responding with the appropriate use of force if necessary. I knew that he could take care of himself, that he would always be fine. Of course, at that time I knew nothing about cops, depression, and suicide.

Now I reverse the *Highway Patrol* DVD and go back to the scene where John begins to pursue the truck in his patrol car. His voice is still firm and calm as he calls in the information. I freeze the DVD. I look at my son. I see his face, a three-quarters view, partly turned toward the camera. He looks through the windshield, his eyes squinting, completely focused on the chase. I see a look of absolute determination bordering on stubbornness, a look he had whenever there was a challenge or problem when he was a child and a young man. I see a man who could never lose his way, who would never want to end his life. My tears begin to flow. But at the same time I feel like I've been on another ride-along with John. I've been with him, close to him, connected to him. I'll take any opportunity I can get to be with him, to put off remembering what happened, to pretend—even for a moment—that it didn't happen.

A week later I'm talking to John Weiss, and I mention that I've watched the DVD. He chuckles and says, "There's a little more to that story." He tells me that the film crew came to Scotts Valley for the reenactment of the chase, and during the filming John accidentally ran over a cat. John never told me about that. I knew about the incident where John ran over the foot of an elderly woman, but maybe he thought I didn't need to know about this other mishap. From what I can gather from John Weiss, John Cahill took a lot of abuse from his friends for running over that cat.

* * *

It's Wednesday morning of Easter week. I wake up intending to work out at the gym, but I can't move, I don't want to move. I've been awake off and on all night, thinking of John in the cartoons, thinking of John in his patrol car, thinking of John with me on the top of Half Dome, thinking of John at my retirement dinner, thinking of John out on that trail all night. This is a day to stay under the covers, to not face the day, to not face my reality, to not face that my rock is gone.

Finally I get up and get in the shower, my other refuge from reality. I'm standing under the hot water, intending to stay there until it runs out. All of a sudden, I think of the title of a book that came out years ago, *Why Bad Things Happen to Good People.* Up until now I've never paid any attention to that book, assuming it was some type of self-help book. In the years before John died I thought it wouldn't be relevant for me. But somewhere at the back of my mind I held onto the title, and this morning, standing in the shower, I know that I want to read it. I step out of the shower, get dressed, jump in my car, and drive to our local bookstore. The store has one paperback copy. I pay for it and bring it home.

I make myself a cup of coffee, sit at the kitchen counter, and begin to read. Rabbi Harold Kushner wrote the book in 1981, after his fourteen-year-old son died. Kushner writes: "God does not cause our misfortunes. Some are caused by bad luck, some are caused by bad people, and some are simply the inevitable consequence of our being human and being mortal, living in a world of inflexible natural laws. The painful things that happen to us are not punishments for our misbehavior, nor are they in any way part of some grand design on God's part." Kushner says we should try to focus on how we respond to our loss. If the death of a loved one makes us bitter and miserable, then our loved one becomes a symbol of despair. If our loss "leads us to explore the limits of our capacity for strength and love," then our loved one is "a witness for the affirmation of life." On this day in 2009, as I sit at my kitchen counter reading these words, I know I'm not there yet, but I know I don't want John to be a symbol of despair.

* * *

On Memorial Day Donna and I are sitting out on the back deck enjoying our morning coffee. I'm thinking of the times when John would be sitting out here with us, and I suddenly realize that it's been two months since I last heard John's "voice." I expect to feel depressed as the thought enters my mind, but instead, inexplicably, I feel comforted. Maybe I'm connecting to the idea of John being in his new life more than I know. I tell Donna what I'm thinking. She looks at me and says, "Maybe he's already told you all the important things." Then her eyes light up, she jumps up excitedly and says, "Go get your journal." I grab my journal from the nightstand in our bedroom, and she goes to her computer in the next room. She has me dictate John's words and the date of each quote. She types these into a Word document, and then she adds a photo of John from her picture file to the document. In it a smiling John sits in a campground with a bottle of New-castle in his hand. On the second page of the document she types a quote from the Book of Wisdom: "The souls of the just are in the hand of God and no torment shall touch them . . . " the reading from John's funeral mass. She prints one copy of the document with John's quotes on one side and the Wisdom passage on the other side. Then she laminates the document and hands it to me. She smiles and says, "Now you can hear him whenever you want, and you can be reminded where he is."

* * *

The next day when I get the mail, there's a beige envelope with a neat, hand-written address in black ink. I smile and my spirits are lifted, because I know from past correspondence that this distinctive handwriting can only belong to John's friend, John Weiss. I don't want to wait until I get upstairs, so I open the envelope in the garage and take out a one-page handwritten note on Scotts Valley Police Department stationery. Weiss wrote, "Dear Brian and Donna, yesterday I was rummaging through one of my art files when I came across an old postcard advertisement for an art show in Santa Cruz. I set the postcard down on my desk, directly in front of the photo of John and me that you gave me, Brian. A bit later in the day I happened to turn over the postcard and discovered a sticky note written to me by Johnny. He had apparently come across the postcard advertisement and he passed it on to me. (The note read: "Brother Weiss, you probably already know about this, but just in case you didn't, here is the info. Let's do some raw fish some-time.") Naturally he would suggest we do a little raw fish. When Johnny and I met he had never eaten sushi. I dragged him down to Mobo Sushi in Santa

Cruz and introduced him to sushi. Before long he was hooked. It's funny that I set the postcard directly beneath Johnny's photo. Needless to say, it made me smile when I discovered the thoughtful note he had written. You raised a remarkable son, indeed."

John Cahill was a remarkable son, but I'm not sure how much credit I deserve for that. I know that John was thoughtful and considerate, but it is comforting and affirming to have his friends tell me that. I'm standing in the garage near the mailbox with this note in my hand, smiling and then crying. I completely forget about the rest of the mail in the box. I open the door to my study, which is just off the garage. I sit at my desk still holding Weiss's note. On the bookshelf to my right is a picture of the two Johns together. It's a headshot of both of them, taken a few years before John died. They've been out in the sun and they have huge smiles on their faces, as if they've pulled off some great feat. John Weiss knew John Cahill pretty well. For him to call John "remarkable" is solid praise.

John Cahill was a remarkable son. He was my son. And now he's gone. I put Weiss's note on the desk in front of me and in this moment I'm close to my John. I'm not hearing him or seeing him, not even thinking his spirit is right here with me, but I'm comforted by the thought of him—my remarkable son indeed.

8

That's Definitely Cahill

In June Donna, LeAnn, and I take John's ashes up to the Tuolumne Gorge in northern Yosemite. John Weiss, Bruce, Alisa, and several of John's other friends join us. After consulting with Kaitlin's therapist, Michele has let us know that the girls will not be joining us. We stay at Evergreen Lodge, near Camp Mather, where my family stayed every summer when I was a kid. The next morning we drive partway up to Hetch Hetchy Reservoir, to a spot about three miles past Mather. We park our cars in a small turn-out area, cross the road, climb up forty or fifty feet, and come out on a flat ledge where there's a beautiful view overlooking the Tuolumne Gorge, a favorite Cahill place.

We all catch our breath and spend a few minutes taking in the vista—groves of pine trees perilously hanging from granite cliffs, the narrow river moving in slow motion two thousand feet below us. I take out the laminated card that Donna made for me, with the passage from the Book of Wisdom on one side and, on the other side, what John—the spirit of John, John-in-his-new-life John—said to me in those moments when I was in bed, in the shower, sitting in the movie theater. This morning when John Weiss and I were getting ready to get into our cars to drive up here—we met in the parking lot in front of the lodge—I told him I was going to read the piece from Scripture and that on the reverse side of the card were some quotes from John. I didn't tell him the messages came to me from John after he died.

Up on top of the gorge I begin to read from the Book of Wisdom. I'm determined not to get emotional, but two lines into the passage my voice begins to quiver. After I shakily finish the Scripture reading, Weiss takes the card from me, turns it over and starts reading the quotes from John aloud. I can tell by the look on his face that he realizes these are words that came from John after he died, messages I got from John between mid-December and the end of March. When I look around I see that LeAnn realizes it too. Donna has a small peaceful smile on her face. The others are looking down, so I can't tell what they're thinking. I hadn't anticipated that anyone would see the quotes from John, and I'm not sure what to expect. Weiss finishes reading John's words. He looks up at me and there's joy on his face. He starts chuckling. He's still looking at me but addresses the entire group, "That's definitely Cahill. That is just the way John spoke and expressed himself." No one else says anything, but Donna catches my eye. She's still smiling.

My hand is shaking as I take a handful of my son's ashes out of the cardboard container. I kneel down on the granite ledge. Donna kneels next to me with her arms around my shoulders, partly to comfort me, partly to make sure I don't fall over the edge of the cliff. I spread some of the ashes on the granite ledge and let the remaining ashes slip through my fingers into the gorge. Without warning, I'm filled with the same horror and guilt I felt last February when it first came to me that I had let John slip through my fingers. It's a feeling that will stay with me for some time.

Then Donna takes out a small silver spoon she brought, scoops up some of John's ashes from the container and pours them onto the granite where she's kneeling. Now I'm holding onto her the way she held onto me. Alisa takes the spoon from Donna, scoops a spoonful of John's ashes from the box and spreads the ashes on the granite ledge next to a small pine tree. John Weiss takes a spoonful of his friend's ashes and lets them blow away, some into the air and some down into the gorge. Bruce and the others do the same. Then LeAnn takes the plastic bag with the remaining ashes out of the cardboard box. She lies down on her stomach at the edge of the cliff and lets the ashes fall down into the gorge. The last of my son's ashes float away.

Then we all sit on the rocks, looking out at the Tuolumne Gorge. We can look straight down two thousand feet and see the dark-green Tuolumne River snake through the gorge. We can look east four miles and see the white concrete O'Shaughnessy Dam and, beyond it, the Hetch Hetchy Reservoir. We can look straight across at the massive granite face of the north side of the gorge, topped by a forest of pine and cedar. My son's spirit lives on, but what's left of his body is in this beautiful place that he loved. I stand up, knowing I'll come back here, knowing John is gone, but hoping that by being here I can be connected to him.

We finally climb back down from the edge of the gorge. Before we get back in our cars, I notice LeAnn is rubbing her head. I ask her if she's okay and she says she's fine but she thinks some dirt must have gotten into her hair during the climb.

When we get back to Evergreen, Alisa takes me aside before we go into the bar. She says, "I have something for you." She goes into her cabin and comes back with a beautiful framed color photograph of Hetch Hetchy that John found in a gallery last year. The picture was shot just before sunrise from the top of O'Shaughnessy Dam, looking east, with the waters of the Hetch Hetchy Reservoir in the foreground. On the left, from the top of the northern cliffs, Wapama Falls drops twelve hundred feet into the reservoir. On the right, on the south side of the cliffs, the thousand-foot-tall Kolama Rock stands in stark profile in the increasing light from the east. In between the cliffs, looking east beyond the reservoir, the sun is still not up, but yellow rays of sunlight are shooting up like wide-beamed searchlights. The light-blue sky is speckled with clouds. The cliffs nearest the dam are still shrouded in partial darkness, but the early sunlight has painted an orange surface on the water of the reservoir.

That picture now hangs over my dresser in our bedroom. I see it every morning when I get up. Each day when I grab my wallet and my car keys from the top of the dresser and put on my wristwatch—John's wristwatch—I soak up the picture. I remember all the times our family was up there, all the times John and I were up there. The dark tones in the picture hint at sadness, but the ascending light suggests hope and definitely a new day. Now every time I gaze into that picture I'm connected to my son—in his new life.

That evening we have drinks around the outdoor fire pit. We hoist more than a few in honor of John Francis Cahill. We go in for dinner and John Weiss and Bruce open up some bottles of James Gang Reserve Cabernet that they brought with them for this time. John always referred to James Gang Reserve as "a very good weeknight red." I'm sitting there with Donna, LeAnn, and John's friends, amidst stories and memories and laughter, feeling the way I felt during memorial gatherings early on after John's death—more like I'm an observer than a participant. But now there's no shock to filter the pain, and I look around the table knowing John is gone, knowing we're here because he's gone, knowing there'll always be pain, there'll always be loss. No matter how much love there is around this table, it can't remove the pain. It can't undo the loss. Then I notice that LeAnn is still rubbing her head.

Later, as Donna and I are walking with her back to our cabins, LeAnn suddenly says, "Oh my God, it's John." We ask her what she means. She looks at us and holds out something in her hand. We can't see it, so she says, "It's John's ashes. I have John's ashes in my hair." Then she holds her head in her hands and we hold her.

* * *

One night in July Donna reads Psalm 95, ". . . God, the rock who saves us
. . ." I'm still not sure about that. Some days later we read Psalm 71: ". . . be
a rock where I can take refuge. . ." A refuge is definitely appealing, but I'm
not completely convinced that God is capable of providing it.

The next morning I'm running errands and driving by a Catholic
church. There's a funeral procession preparing to depart from the church.
I suddenly see twenty motorcycle officers lined up on their motorcycles,
two by two, on the street, preparing to lead the procession to the cemetery.
I think of the motorcycle officers who led John's funeral. I want to turn
around, go home, and get under the covers. A few days later, I hear John
Lennon's "Beautiful Boy" on the radio, and all I can do is cry.

Since John died I cry at the drop of a hat. In *Lament for a Son*, Nicholas
Wolterstorff writes about how he felt after the death of his son, "I shall look
at the world through tears."

During this time I'm aware that with all the pain, horror, and depression I'm experiencing, I'm still not feeling any anger toward John for what
he did. Janet has told me that the anger may come, and that if it does I
should acknowledge it, try to focus on John's new life, and release the anger.
But I'm not angry, at least not yet. I wonder whether, if I felt anger, it would
reduce some of the pain and horror. Is it a zero-sum game, or would I just
feel worse?

One night in August, nine months after John's death, I'm watching the
DVD of his life. I've been doing this pretty regularly, trying to hold onto
the past, trying to stay connected. Suddenly a new thought comes to me.
I freeze the video on the picture of John and me, taken at the top of Half
Dome in 2002, and I sit there remembering what I heard John say during
the first few months after he died: "You have to be in the new life, and then
it won't hurt so much." Even then I knew he was saying that I had to start
thinking of him in *his* new life.

In the moment when I heard—took in—John saying that, I had a general sense of comfort, but it was short-lived. I had the same reaction when
Donna said that John went right to God; it was a briefly comforting thought,
but it wasn't able to offset the horror and pain. But now, as I sit here looking
at the picture of John standing next to me with his arm around me on Half
Dome, I realize that lately the words "new life" have been more and more
on my mind, not just because that's what John said to me, but because it's
a way to explain to myself, to remind myself, a way to affirm that his spirit,
his soul, is not gone. His body is definitely gone. In that way he has been
irrevocably removed from this life, and on my bad days that's all I can grasp.
But on the lighter days, the days when I'm able to focus on John's spirit—on
this "new life" of his—I'm able to realize, or at least argue to myself, that

it makes no sense that John's spirit, his essence, would not continue; that it makes no sense that the spark of life and love that was so clearly in him would be permanently extinguished just because his body is gone.

The life of the spirit is not finite the way the life of the body is. I realize that if I didn't have a basic sense of that concept I might never have been able to hear John during those first few months after his death. Could I be fooling myself about hearing John? Of course I could. Freud and many other great thinkers would dismiss me as delusional. But I can't let go of the reality of the love that was in John, the spark that was in him, the vitality that was in him, the goodness that was in him—these are not finite; these are not limited; they have no expiration date.

In *Stations of the Heart* Richard Lischer struggles with feeling disconnected from his departed son. Then he realizes, "The dead are completed beings who are no longer subject to the limitations of time and space and are therefore available to us across the entire surface of our lives."

I play the rest of the video, still crying as I see my son in his old life. But from this point forward I will watch the DVD less and less frequently. I won't feel disloyal or guilty or disconnected, because he's in my thoughts most of the time anyway. But I will begin to focus, a little more steadily, a little more consistently, on John in his new life, on being connected to him in his new life.

＊ ＊ ＊

In mid-October Donna is visiting her parents in Pennsylvania, and I decide to drive up to Hetch Hetchy for the day. When my dad drove us up here after the war in his 1941 Ford, it was a six-hour trip on mostly two-lane roads. Today the trip takes three hours. I remember my childhood experience of the long drive out of the Bay Area and across the Central Valley. When we started to climb up Highway 120 into the Sierras, my sister and I were always torn between our excitement about being on vacation and our fear of getting carsick on the winding road. As I drive up 120 today, heading toward the northern boundary of Yosemite, I remember that childhood sense of anticipation and excitement. Today I'm driving up here to be with my son, not literally, but with his spirit. It's a different type of anticipation and there's no excitement. But there is comfort, a sense of connection. I'll settle for that.

I pass Evergreen Lodge and Camp Mather and drive up to the edge of the Tuolumne Gorge, where we spread John's ashes. I park the car, cross the road, and begin to climb up the rocks to get to the top of the ledge that overlooks the gorge. I'm halfway to the top when I realize I'm not climbing very fast. It's only a fifty-foot climb, and there are enough rocks and tree branches to grab as handholds, so it's not that difficult. But I'm breathing hard, and I remember I was breathing hard when I climbed up here a few months ago with everyone to spread John's ashes. I didn't notice then that I was laboring, but today I do. It dawns on me that as I get older this climb will get harder and the time may come when I won't be able to make it to the top. Then I think that what is left of my son's body is up here. I want to bring Krissy and Kaitlin up here. I want to keep coming back here. So I'll keep climbing up here until my last breath, even if it kills me. As I grab for a tree branch and continue to climb, I find myself thinking that if I did die sometime in the future climbing up here, it would be a fitting way to go—I would be close to John.

I get to the top, walk over to the edge of the cliff, sit down on a rock, and catch my breath. I look at the spot on the ledge where we spread John's ashes. There is no trace of them. They have blown away, some into the gorge, some into the air, some into the trees. But he's here. Even some of his ashes are probably here, although today I can't see them. I can't see any part of him. I can't even hear him today. But he's here. I can feel his presence.

In his study of grief, *The Other Side of Sadness*, George Bonanno writes, "Research shows that some bereaved have sensed the presence of a deceased loved one to a profound extent." One of Bonanno's patients wrote, "I lost his body, but not his soul. He's with me every day." I'm beginning to know what she means.

I sit on the edge of the cliff with my legs hanging over the side. I tell John how much I miss him and how much I love him. I promise him that I will try to live the rest of my life in his honor, try to make him a symbol of love and life and hope and trust in God. I ask him to help me be a good husband, a good father, a good grandfather, a good friend. The weather is overcast. So am I. But this is still the most beautiful place in the world for me.

I look down at the Tuolumne River where John and I fished years ago. I remember that last year at this time John talked about the two of us taking Kaitlin on her first white water trip in the summer of 2009. We also talked about future fishing trips to the high country for us, although we agreed that because we were getting soft we would go in on horseback rather than backpacking. I sit here and realize we'll never have those experiences.

I look up to my right, to the east, and I see O'Shaughnessy Dam and Hetch Hetchy Reservoir in the distance. I think of John and me backpacking six miles around the far side of Hetch Hetchy up to Rancheria Creek that time the bears got all our food. Kaitlin will never have those kinds of experiences with her dad, never be up here with him in this place he loved.

I don't even know if Kaitlin would want to be backpacking and fishing up here, but it doesn't matter, because the choice has been taken away from her. The opportunity to be with her dad in the mountains has been permanently rescinded.

All of a sudden I realize I need to get away from this place. I climb back down to the road, get back in my car, and head home. I don't stop at Evergreen for a drink. I don't stop to eat. Anger, resentment, the unfairness of it all keeps me awake and alert on the road.

A few days later I learn that the Bug Brothers, John's dive group, have taken the rest of John's ashes out to the Channel Islands, his favorite place to dive. It turns out they scattered his ashes on the same day I was up at Hetch Hetchy.

* * *

Two months later I'm sitting at my desk working on issues relating to the probate of John's estate. It's boring but necessary work, and I have to get it to our attorney soon. I'm distracted and I keep thinking about what Janet told me about not being able to save John, that even if I had known all about cops and suicide I couldn't have stopped John from doing what he did. I'm struck now by a phrase she used. I remember her sitting next to me on the sofa in her office and saying, "From the point of time that John made up his mind, nothing could have stopped him."

But what if I had known that depression could lead cops to suicide *before* John made up his mind? What if I had told John about that then? What if I had told him he could get frustrated when he couldn't control things in his life the way he controlled things as a cop? What if I had told him that because his problems in life can't be taken care of as quickly as the problems he faced as a cop, he might start to think that his problems would never end? What if I told him he was wrong about all of that, that if he started thinking that way it just meant that his perspective was distorted? And what if I had told him all that before he started to despair, before he lost his way, before he stopped listening?

As I sit there at my desk, I don't know the answers to any of these questions. I remember Janet telling me I couldn't have stopped him. And I know I have to face the reality that it doesn't matter anyway. It's too late for John. But then I think about other cops and their fathers, and I think about what my friend Rita told me in December about my needing to find a way to honor John.

Suddenly I don't even see the probate documents spread out in front of me. For the first time since John died, I feel a spark of excitement. I know what I want to do. I don't have a clue how to go about it, and I don't have the slightest idea what form it will take, but I know I want to help cops. I want to help them avoid doing what John did. I want to help their fathers avoid feeling and experiencing what I'm still feeling and experiencing. And I want to help their mothers and their spouses and partners and brothers and sisters. I want to help their children. I want to help cops *before* they get depressed, before they start to despair, before they lose their way, before they stop listening. Before it's too late.

I call Janet and ask her if I can come and see her. A day later I'm sitting in her waiting room. As I sit there people come in and the waiting room fills up. I wonder if any of them are here to talk about how they will honor their loved ones.

Janet brings me into her office and offers me the Kleenex box. I tell her I won't need it today. I tell her that I'm thinking of volunteering in the area of suicide prevention for police officers. I would tell John's story and talk about what's been learned about cops and depression and what they need to do to avoid what happened to John. I tell her that I know I have a lot to learn, but this is what I want to do to honor John.

Janet looks at me. I can tell that she knows she can't stop me from this path. She reminds me that there will be a price to pay for this kind of work, because I'll be continuously revisiting the horror of John's death. She insists that I not start anything for at least another year. She also tells me that if I do this work, the reality of John's suicide will hit deeper but I will pull out faster. The more I acknowledge the pain, she says, the more my mind and body can work together to heal. As I leave, she hugs me and says, "You'll have to be careful, but this is a good thing."

It will be a year and a half before I give my first suicide prevention presentation to San Francisco police officers. Janet was right: I will have to be careful, but it will turn out to be a very good thing.

9

A Sense of God

It's a weekday a little less than a year after John's death and I'm running some errands. On the spur of the moment I decide to visit my mother's grave at Holy Cross Cemetery, just south of San Francisco. I haven't gone there since John died. My mom Margaret passed away in 1967, and my dad married Ruth three years later.

I pick up some flowers at the shop across from the entrance gate of the cemetery and drive up to the section where Margaret O'Leary Cahill is buried. I get out of the car, walk over, and place the flowers on her headstone. I start to tell her what happened to John, but then I realize she already knows. My mom was pretty sick when John was born, but I know that she and her grandson would have been joined at the hip if they had had time together in this life. As I stand there I imagine my mom smiling and saying that she and John are making up for lost time now.

On my way home from the cemetery I drive by a Catholic church that I've never noticed before. Making another spur of the moment decision, I park the car in the church parking lot and go in. It's a large Spanish-style structure built in the late fifties, with simple clean lines. The cream-colored walls are interspersed with stained-glass windows depicting different scenes in the life of Mary. The ceiling consists of large wooden beams running the length of the church. Behind the altar is a massive freestanding wooden crucifix. The early afternoon fall sunlight is streaming through the windows. It's warm, quiet, and peaceful here. I'm the only one in the church.

I sit in a back pew, not really praying, just sitting there enjoying the warmth and quiet, appreciating the peace, trying to be in God's presence. I'm not as angry with God now for letting my son take his life. I'm not doing any more silent screaming. And while I'm not sure God is my refuge, I'm no longer actively questioning His competence. I'm just trying to have some kind of connection. I sit there for five or six minutes, and then I hear something. What I hear will change my world view, my faith, and give me an entirely new sense of God. And, although I won't always be able to hold onto it, it will give me a realization that God loves me in spite of my failures and I can trust that love.

I hear a voice say, "I *am* your rock. Trust me. You will be fine. You will see him. You will live your life in honor of him."

I hear the voice the way I've heard John's voice: inside my head, clear, not imagined. But there's something different this time from when I heard John's voice. At first I think this voice is somehow more of an inner voice. But then I realize I'm not hearing a voice at all. I'm taking in the words. I'm absorbing them. And they're coming from within me. But they're not coming from me. I think the words are coming from God.

First I'm startled, then I'm comforted and grateful. I start to weep, silently.

I sit there, not wanting to move, not wanting to lose the wonderful sense of comfort I suddenly have, comfort that I haven't felt even when I've heard John. I want to hold onto this feeling, not let anything diminish it, not have any doubts about what just happened.

Then, before I can head off the thought, it crosses my mind that maybe I've imagined God speaking to me. But this thought, this doubt, doesn't take over; it doesn't destroy my sense of comfort. And then I think about how since John's death there have been a number of hints telling me that God has been present in my life. I've heard John's voice telling me that he is with God. There have been repeated references to God as my rock in the Psalms that Donna and I have read in our morning and evening prayers. And Donna's prayers and insights into God's love over these last few months have been constant and steady, not always consciously registered by me, but not always ignored or resisted. And as I reflect on all these hints, these signs, I relax, thinking there's a certain logic, a certain flow, a certain build-up to what just happened.

The afternoon light is fading, and the church is getting dark. I haven't moved from my back pew. I'm still savoring the comfort of what I've experienced, wanting to affirm that it was real, not imagined, not fantasized.

Now, as I write this, looking back on that moment I know it's within the realm of possibility that I conjured up this conveniently specific, divine announcement. Nietzsche and other nonbelieving philosophers maintain that all religious experience is human projection—self-created, unconscious, comfort-seeking rationalization. Obviously a lot of that goes on. But in my case I think it's just as likely that after all the hints and signs He's given me—signs I *know* I haven't conjured, any more than I've created this moment here in this church—God thinks I'm such a poor listener and slow learner that He had to resort to a basic, direct, unmistakable message.

And I'm not just a slow learner and a poor listener. I'm a father whose son committed suicide, a father who's immobilized by horror and pain, a father who's overwhelmed with a sense of failure, a father who is down, depressed, at the bottom of the sinkhole. And maybe this is what it took for me to finally pay attention to God. In *A Jesuit Guide to Almost Everything*, James Martin writes, "God is able to reach us because our defenses are lowered."

I've always easily and perhaps thoughtlessly believed in God, though if I'm honest, until my divorce and then my son's suicide, I hadn't given the issue of faith much attention. Like C.S. Lewis, I have wondered what kind of God allows the pain, chaos, and destruction that are rampant in this life. I've come to at least a partial understanding of the implications of free will and the existence of evil, and in the spirit of Rabbi Kushner I've tried to make sense of the world's pain and evil. In *A Grief Observed*, Lewis writes, "You never know how much you really believe anything until its truth or falsehood becomes a matter of life and death to you." As the father of a son who put a bullet through his temple, I am no longer a spectator with a minor amount of scar tissue from previous pain. Now I'm inalterably linked to pain and evil and death, as a participant and as a survivor, with no way to avoid an examination of what I believe.

I don't pretend to have a clear picture or understanding of God—of course, nobody does. Michael Novak, in *No One Sees God,* writes that God "is beyond any human frequency. He is outside our range, divine." God is certainly outside my range. I definitely don't see God. I'm not sure I can even glimpse God. Perhaps the most I will ever be able to do is have a sense of God at times, to feel God's presence, to feel God's love. And I will continue to ask why God let my son take his life. And I will still have bad days, days where my faith seems to fade. But I have—at least once, I think, in the back pew of a church on a late fall afternoon—received a message from God, a sense of God.

* * *

Once, on a white water rafting trip on the upper Tuolumne, John and I were camped for the night, drinking beer and watching the sun drop below the canyon walls. I told him that whenever I was up here I felt God's presence. John didn't spend much time on matters of God, but when he did he was a thoughtful agnostic. He looked at me, smiled tolerantly, and said, "I know you feel God's presence up here, because every time we're up here you tell me that." I waited for him to keep talking. "You may be right about God," he said after a long pause, "and you're certainly right about the beauty of this place. But I don't believe we can prove or disprove God's existence. I always listen to everything you say, but at this point in my life, between family and work, there's not much room for theology." He looked at me and smiled again—a boyish, let's-change-the-subject smile—and said, "How about a second beer?" I reached in the cooler, cracked open two more beers, and changed the subject.

As the light faded and I looked at my son and sipped my beer, I remembered another conversation John and I had a few years back. We were having lunch when John asked me if I was disappointed that he was not religious. He said that he always respected my beliefs and he loved that I never pushed him, but he worried that he had let me down. I looked at my son over the lunch table and told him that I could never be disappointed in him and that he could never let me down by not having beliefs similar to mine. I told him I would never push him, because I saw the way he lived his life. I told him how much I respected him.

Years ago I had read *The Anonymous Christian*, an essay by the German theologian Karl Rahner. Rahner says there are many people who are neither believers in God nor followers of Jesus Christ, but who live their lives in such a way that God's grace is manifest in their values and their behavior. Rahner maintains that when they die they go right to God. As I write this, I know that there are and have been many good, non-religious people with integrity in this life. My son Ed is one of them. John was one of them. I believe John went right to God. I wouldn't want any part of a God who wouldn't take my son into His arms.

* * *

After John's death, I read Michael Krasny's *Spiritual Envy,* a probing and honest account of an agnostic's search for God. John Cahill would have liked this book. Krasny, a well-known commentator on National Public Radio, is honest enough to acknowledge the consolation of faith, but even more honest about his need to question everything about faith. And Julian Barnes, another thoughtful agnostic, writes in *Nothing to be Frightened Of,* "I don't believe in God, but I miss him."

I'm not an agnostic, but I'm no longer an automatic believer. For me, Kierkegaard's famous "leap to faith" is an appealing concept. The idea of an act of faith as a leap makes sense to me. On good days I leap with a sense of security. On bad days I leap hoping there will be some kind of God-created net to catch me. And the leap—the act of faith—has to be repeated regularly. C.S. Lewis says, "Relying on God has to start over every day as if nothing yet had been done." In *The Habit of Being*, Flannery O'Connor writes, "Faith comes and goes. It rises and falls like the tides of an invisible ocean. If it is presumptuous to think that faith will stay with you forever, it is just as presumptuous to think that unbelief will."

Anyone who wants to can find philosophers or theologians to help them justify their disbelief or shore up their belief in God. But it is neither the comfort of spiritual opium nor the avoidance of despair that ultimately tilts me toward faith. In spite of evil, chaos, war, and poverty, I see in so many individuals an essence of love, energy, endurance, commitment, passion, compassion, creativity . . . and I can't avoid the thought that there must be a source for this essence, this spark. I believe that spark, that essence that was in John, is still present somewhere—*is* John, continues to be John.

My faith, both before and especially after John's suicide, has been challenged, but it's also been bolstered by, for example, the experience I had in that church just south of San Francisco, when I heard—felt, sensed—God talking to me. There have been other moments, too, when I had intense experiences of God's presence. As I told John, every time I go up to the edge of the Tuolumne Gorge, I feel God's presence, and I find it impossible to believe that this beautiful combination of granite, water, trees, and light, no matter how many millions of years in the making, does not have a divine origin.

I've been to Yad Vashem, the Holocaust Memorial in Jerusalem, which some see as a symbol of God's absence but where I and many others have breathed in God's presence. At the Memorial to the Deportees, I read a poem that was found on the wall of a cellar near Cologne, France, where a Jewish family had been hiding from the Gestapo:

> I believe in the sun, though it is late in rising.
> I believe in love, though it is absent.
> I believe in God, though he is silent.

I have been on a hillside in Medjugorje, Bosnia, where the Blessed Mother has been appearing since 1981; this is the most prayerful place I've ever been, and for me and millions of others, God's presence is palpable there. I went there with my wife in 2004, in the aftermath of the tragic and bloody breakup of Yugoslavia. I didn't experience any miracles as others claim, but on that hillside and in the crowded local church jammed with thousands of people singing and praying in English, French, German, Italian, Spanish and Croatian, the sense of God's presence was overwhelming.

I've been to Wednesday Vespers during Lent in San Francisco's Castro district, at Most Holy Redeemer Church, a welcoming community for

Catholic gays and lesbians since the early eighties, a convenient target for homophobes and fundamentalists, and a holy place of tested faith where God is always present. I've experienced God's presence in that church.

And, especially, I have experienced God's presence in the chapel at San Quentin prison.

10

Where Souls are Locked Down and Where Souls are Lifted Up

ONE SUNDAY MORNING IN June of 2009, I come into the prison and walk into the chapel about a half-hour before Mass starts. I've learned to come early because a number of men always want to talk to me, as they would with any visitor from the outside. As I pass through the vestibule of the chapel, Ron, one of the inmates, comes up to me. He shakes my hand but he's not smiling. He asks if we can talk. He leads me over to the back corner of the chapel. "I had another parole hearing this week," he tells me. He looks at me with sadness and a hint of anger, but also resignation. "I was denied," he says in a low voice.

Ron has been eligible for parole but has previously been denied twice. He was one of the first guys to greet me when I came back to San Quentin after John's death. He's a year older than I am, grew up in San Francisco and went to one of the local Catholic high schools here. In prison he has been a participant in AA, attends Mass regularly, and is active in spiritual retreats and discussion groups through the Catholic chapel.

"This time I thought I had a chance," he tells me.

I stand there, not knowing what to say.

Then Ron says something that floors me. He puts his hand on my arm and tells me, "I'd still like to get out, but I realize I may not. I learned about the denial on Tuesday. By last night I was finally able to say to myself that if it's God's will that I live out my life in here, then I'll try to live that life as well as I can, trusting Him and accepting His will."

I look at this man. I don't know if he will get out. But I think that God really is present in this place of isolation and punishment and suffering. And I also sense that through Ron God is trying to speak to me, to be present to me, to help me accept my suffering, to help me live out the rest of my life

93

as well as I can. I tell Ron I'm sorry and how much I respect his faith. And then it dawns on me that Ron is far more accepting of God's will than I am.

* * *

On a Saturday a few weeks later, some of the men at the prison put on a day of reflection and prayer in the chapel. I'm there along with a few other volunteers. The theme of the day is restorative justice, and the topic is forgiveness. The main speaker is a woman whose son was murdered ten years ago. She talks about how over time she was able to forgive her son's killers. After her talk we break into small groups, and I find myself sitting next to an African-American inmate in his mid-forties who's doing twenty-five to life for murder. His name is Khaleel and he usually attends Muslim services, but he also periodically comes to Catholic services. When it's his time to share, he starts to tell the group that he hopes the family of his victim can eventually forgive him. Then he starts to sob and says, "But even if they would forgive me, I can never forgive myself for what I did."

One of the other men in the group, Ray, says, "I know what you mean. I used to feel that way. But I finally learned that in spite of all the bad stuff I did in my life, in spite of my failures, in spite of my crimes, God continues to love me, and He has forgiven me. So I have to forgive myself." Ray looks hard at Khaleel and says, "God has forgiven you, so you have to forgive yourself."

Khaleel nods, still crying, taking in what Ray said. A year later I will run into Khaleel again. He will tell me that the sister of the man he murdered came to visit him and forgave him, and that he was finally able to forgive himself. He will look at me, smile a small peaceful smile, and say, "I still have to serve my time, but God is amazing."

Now, as the restorative justice session ends, Khaleel walks away. I stand there and think of my own failures—the failure of my first marriage, my failures as a father, especially my failure to protect John, the fact that I let him slip through my fingers. I missed all the signs as John was struggling at the end. Donna and Janet would say I did the best I could and there is nothing to forgive. I'm not so sure. I'm happy for Ray and other guys here who have found true peace in self-forgiveness. I myself am still a work in progress.

* * *

It's a Sunday in early October and I'm at San Quentin for Mass. The chapel is full of guys, which tells me there are no football games of interest on this morning. There are about a dozen volunteers from the outside present. As

Mass begins and Father Barber and the altar servers walk up the aisle, the inmate choir sings a song focusing on God's love and grace. Father Barber opens Mass with a greeting and blessing. Then there's a brief segment where we reflect on our failings and ask God for forgiveness. A song or prayer praising God follows this. By now everyone is settled down and the atmosphere in the chapel is one of quiet reflection, the perfect mood to listen to the word of God. One of the inmates walks up the aisle to the podium on the side of the altar and begins the first reading.

All of a sudden, a loud siren goes off somewhere outside the chapel. Two correctional officers come rushing in and announce that all inmates have to head back to their cells. There's been a violent, gang-related incident in the Adjustment Center and the entire prison is on lockdown. I glance at some of the guys I know. I'm shocked and puzzled, but they shrug their shoulders, not at all surprised or shocked. The inmate beside me smiles sadly and whispers, "That's life in San Quentin." The men walk out of the chapel and head back to their cellblocks.

Father Barber invites the rest of us, the outside volunteers, to come up and stand around the altar. We go on with the Mass, finishing the readings. Father Barber reads the gospel, and then, rather than giving his planned sermon, he looks at us and says, "Anything can happen here, and none of us is in control. Let's pray for whoever is involved in the incident at the Adjustment Center. And let's pray for all the men in the Adjustment Center, for those on death row, and for all the men who had to leave the chapel this morning."

We pray silently and then the Mass continues. From where I'm standing on the altar I can look down the aisle, through the chapel doors, directly across the courtyard to the stark, beige, three-story exterior of the Adjustment Center which runs the length of the courtyard. The building consists of three tiers of isolation cells. Barred windows on each tier run the length of the building. When you're standing in the courtyard, depending on the light, you can look through the windows and see the solid metal doors of all the cells, each with a small, shatterproof panel of glass.

The Adjustment Center is the most secure, tightly guarded unit in San Quentin and serves two purposes. All prisoners who are newly condemned to death go the Adjustment Center, and, after a period of time, if they don't cause any problems, they're transferred to East Block, the main death row section of the prison. The other inmates in the Adjustment Center are those deemed too violent or out of control to be in the main population. All of the Adjustment Center inmates spend most of their time in their cells with little human contact.

I stand on the altar, continuing to look out at the Adjustment Center. It's not that I think those inmates shouldn't be there, safely locked in their isolation cells, but at this moment I'm struck by the contrast in the purpose of these two buildings, no more than fifty yards apart: the AC, where souls are locked down, and the chapel, where souls are lifted up. I'm beginning to realize that this is an environment where grace and evil are in a contest; and while God is present here, sometimes you have to search hard to find Him.

* * *

On a Tuesday night I enter the prison and come into the chapel, this time not knowing what to expect. The two volunteers who facilitate the regular Tuesday night spirituality group have invited me to participate. It's a little after six and the inmates have been released from their cellblocks for evening program. A dozen inmates are sitting in a circle of chairs just in front of the pews closest to the altar, along with two volunteers, both of whom have been coming to San Quentin for the last twenty years. One is a former priest and the other is a retired corporate executive.

One of the inmates says a prayer, and then the volunteer who's facilitating tonight introduces me to the group. I know most of the men from being with them on Sundays, and most of them know about John. The theme tonight is God's forgiveness, and the facilitator reads a passage from Scripture, Psalm 103: "As far as east is from the west, so far has He removed our transgressions from us." Each member of the group, both inmates and volunteers, takes a turn commenting and reflecting on the meaning of the passage. Clint, a tall, gray-haired, middle-aged inmate sitting across from me, tells us that as a teenager he killed a man. He spent the first twenty years in prison not just trying to survive, but also convinced that God could never forgive him for what he did. But through the friendship, support, and advice of a former prison chaplain, he came to realize that God did forgive him. He looks up and says, "It took me a long time to figure it out, but that's what God does. God loves. God forgives." Then he brushes away a tear and says quietly, "I finally realized that if God forgave me, then I needed to forgive myself. I still need to do the time for what I did, but I'm in a far better place now than I was before." The men nod, and a few more of them tell their stories.

I sit there that first Tuesday night, realizing that though I've come as a volunteer to help these men, I need to be here. I need to face my own remorse, gain insight, confront my pain, and hold on to my faith. After the fifth or sixth man speaks about trying to forgive himself because God has forgiven him, I finally realize that this is what I have to do too. I have to forgive myself for not saving John, for not seeing that my son was slipping away. This is not a brand-new idea, and it will be a work in progress for me, but here in San Quentin I can be reminded of God's forgiveness, and I can learn from the example of these men—from their remorse, their insight, their humility, their surrender, and their faith.

On another Tuesday evening the group discusses Matthew 25, the description of the Last Judgment: " . . . I was hungry and you fed me, naked and you clothed me, in prison and you visited me . . . " Each man reflects on what the passage means. At the end of the session a tough, intelligent, deeply spiritual "lifer" looks up and says, "I think it means if you're screwing over your brother, you're screwing over God." Matthew, or whoever wrote that passage, couldn't have said it better or more succinctly.

A month later it's my turn to pick the Scripture passage for discussion. My two colleagues aren't able to make it tonight so I'm my own. Only eight men have shown up. I'm a little nervous, so I pick something familiar. I read out loud from Psalm 62: "God alone is my rock and my salvation." This is what Donna read as part of our night prayers the night of the day we found out John was gone. Then I read from Psalm 31: "You are my rock and my refuge." This was part of our night prayers on the day of John's funeral.

I ask the guys to share their thoughts about these readings. A few guys say they like the reference to God as rock: solid, dependable. Finally Tony, a youthful-looking fifty-year-old lifer, looks at me and says, "These readings seem to have real meaning for you." I sit there in the circle, fighting back tears. The men all know what happened to John, and most of them look down at the floor. When I can talk I say, "John was my rock and I was his rock."

Tony is still looking at me as if he has something to say, and I ask him what the readings mean to him. He takes a long breath and says, "I did a lot of stupid things when I first came into prison, and I spent a lot of time in lockdown. I remember a long stretch in the special housing unit in Pelican Bay. I had a Bible and I read the Psalms. The idea of God as my rock got me through that terrible time."

I walk out of San Quentin that night trying to hold onto the thought that God is my rock and He is getting me through *my* terrible time.

* * *

On November 2 I go over to San Quentin for the Feast of All Souls, the day that the Church remembers all those who have died. My friends Lorenzo, Ron, and Dwayne greet me as I come into the chapel. Another inmate, Brad, a soft-spoken, serious man in his late forties, comes up and gives me a hug.

Brad is an active participant in the restorative justice group, and like Lorenzo, Ron, and Dwayne, he's on a serious faith journey.

When Brad was nineteen he was working as a grocery clerk. An older friend told him he was planning to rob the store after it closed; all Brad had to do was let him in the front door. Brad didn't know how to say no so he agreed. On a late Saturday night Brad left the door ajar. The assistant store manager unexpectedly showed up, confronted Brad's friend, and Brad's friend shot him. Because of Brad's role in the crime, he was convicted of second-degree murder and sentenced to twenty years to life.

When Mass begins, Ron gets up to do the first reading. It's Chapter Three from the Book of Wisdom: "The souls of the just are in the hand of God and no torment shall touch them . . . " I'm trying not to cry, remembering the first time I heard that reading—at my son's funeral.

Father Barber reads the gospel and gives his homily, and then Brad gets up to do the Prayers of the Faithful, where the congregation prays for those who are ill or have special intentions. Because it is All Souls Day, Brad reads from a list of individuals who have died in the past, people known by the men who go to Mass here at San Quentin. He reads a number of names, then pauses, looks up, makes eye contact with me, and says, "John Francis Cahill." I sit there, hating that my son's name is on the All Souls Day list but comforted that he's being remembered.

After Mass a number of guys come up to me. They don't say anything, but each of them gives me a hug. I look at these men, no longer surprised by their compassion, no longer surprised at experiencing God's grace in this place. By now it's clear to me that I come to this place, not just to give comfort to these men, but to receive comfort from them.

1 1

Officer John Cahill,
Badge Number 3357

IT'S DECEMBER 3, 2009, the first anniversary of my son's suicide. We know we need to get away. After Mass Donna and I are driving up the Mendocino coast on Highway One. This part of California's north coast, two hours north of San Francisco, is a combination of gray-blue ocean, rocky coastline, and high mountain ridges covered with Monterey pines. I'm driving on this winding two-lane road, so Donna's enjoying the scenery more than I am. But I'm not feeling depressed, not even feeling the heaviness which is my normal default mood when I'm not mired in the horror of a year ago.

We drive through a number of hamlets that hug the coast—Manchester, Elk, and Albion—and finally, just as the sun is beginning to sink, we arrive at our destination: Little River Inn, just below the town of Mendocino. Our room is in the wing farthest from the main lobby, and it has a clear view of the ocean. Before we walk over to the hotel restaurant for dinner we break out a bottle of John's favorite wine, a Tobin James Zinfandel. We sit on our hotel room's small deck and look out at the dark ocean and the gray and black sky tinged with a hint of receding orange light. We toast John Francis Cahill.

Donna goes in to get ready for dinner and I pour a second glass of the Zin. Ed told me last week that just because today was John's anniversary, I wasn't required to grovel in pain. He was right, and for the moment I'm not.

The next day Donna and I explore Mendocino, a town full of Victorian houses perched on a headland surrounded by the Pacific. Donna checks out the art studios and knickknack shops and I check out the bakery, the bookstore, and a couple of the bars. John would approve of how we're observing his anniversary, I think.

The next day we drive back home through Mendocino and Sonoma wine country, having had enough of winding coastal roads. Just before we get to Highway 101, which will take us south to San Francisco, I think of being on the massage table a few days after John's funeral and hearing him tell me to relax and enjoy the massage. I tell Donna. We look at each other and smile, trying to hold onto the mood of the last couple of days, trying to remember that what we're really celebrating is the first anniversary of John's new life.

* * *

Then it's December 9, the anniversary of John's funeral. Donna and I are going to a candlelight vigil at the Center for Living with Dying near San Jose, where my counselor Janet Childs works. Each year Janet puts on a ceremony honoring those who have died and providing support for those who survive them. Usually about two to three hundred people attend. I've been many times to Janet's office on the upper floor of a two-story office building, but I've never noticed the large conference room on the building's first floor.

Donna and I enter the conference room a few minutes before the program starts. Rows of chairs are arranged auditorium-style, and people are beginning to take their seats. At the front of the room are two long tables with a podium and a microphone between them. On either side of the podium, running the length of each table, are five rows of ten-inch-tall, three-inch-wide candles in clear glass jars. The candles are in various shades of blue—some dark navy blue, some deep turquoise, some almost aquamarine. On a small separate table are eight or ten larger candles, each one about the size of a roll of paper towels. Behind that table is a sign that says "Community Candles." As I sit down with Donna in the fourth row from the front on the left side, I wonder what the candles are all about.

Janet opens the evening with welcoming comments and a brief description of the mission and services of the Center for Living with Dying. Then she talks about the purpose of the evening: to let go of the trauma and pain of the loss of our loved ones without losing our love, memories, and sense of closeness to those we have lost. We are also here to experience the power of community and shared grief and to honor those we have lost. Janet is as calm, compassionate, and supportive in this large group setting as she is in our individual sessions.

I was reluctant to come to this gathering, fearful that it would bring me back to the horror and pain of a year ago, but during my last appointment Janet reassured me that it would be a good experience for me, and

Donna gave me no choice but to get in the car with her and drive down here tonight. I listen to Janet speak and begin to calm down.

I look around the room. Everyone here has lost a loved one, but I find myself trying to spot the parents, the ones who are here not just because they lost a son or daughter, but because they are still trying to figure out how it came to be that their child has not outlived them, how it came to be that all the rules of the universe have been shattered. There are tears on some faces; other people have looks that tell me they've been to this ceremony before. Then I take a second look around the room, wondering how many of the people here have lost kids to suicide, how many fathers feel, like me, that they let their son or daughter slip through their fingers, that they missed the signs, that they failed to protect their child.

Janet had mentioned that not all the folks here are suicide survivors, and I'm also wondering if those folks might be feeling slightly better than the suicide survivors, because their child or loved one was taken from them rather than choosing to leave. Then I realize that even if John had died in the line of duty or from an illness, I would still be here, still feeling his loss, perhaps not taking on as much self-blame, but still aching at the hole in my life. We are all here because someone we love has died. Tonight it doesn't matter how it happened. No one's feeling better than anyone else.

At one of our recent meetings Janet told me there's a keynote speaker at each of these annual events, and that John's girlfriend Alisa was going to be the speaker tonight. Alisa also sees Janet for counseling and told Janet she wanted to speak. I've been feeling ambivalent about Alisa being tonight's keynote speaker. There's no way that at this point I could stand up and talk about my son and what happened, so on one hand I'm glad that Alisa is able to do it. But I also think that *I'm* supposed to be the one to speak about John—I'm his father, after all—and I'd rather wait until I'm ready to do that and not have anyone else talk about John up there.

Alisa walks up to the podium. She's wearing pressed jeans, low heels, a white blouse, and a black leather jacket. As she turns and faces us the look on her face is determined, resolute. I know she's been devastated by John's death. She takes a deep breath and speaks into the microphone. "We were together less than a year, but John Cahill was the love of my life." She describes how they met in a wine bar in Santa Cruz. I remember the moment when John told me about Alisa. He was low-key about it, but I knew he was pleased. So was I, because I thought it would be a step in his moving forward, in his healing.

Alisa talks about her relationship with John and about the special relationship there is between cops and nurses—fellow first responders. She describes that last day when John brought her lunch. He was calm—still down, but not acting any differently than he had been. She says that she invited him to come to her place that night to share some leftovers for dinner and that he said he would bring a new bottle of wine he wanted to try. Alisa looks up at the audience. "I loved John. I knew he was going through a rough time, but I didn't know how rough." She pauses and takes a deep breath. "I know that everyone in this room is feeling the pain of losing a loved one." I look around. There's a noticeable reaction in the room, a feeling of people relaxing, releasing tension. I see some heads nodding, some tears, but there's also almost a sense of comfort throughout the room, throughout this community of grievers. Alisa walks back and sits next to us. I hug her, grateful that she was strong enough to get up there and honor my son.

Then Janet explains the "Community Candles." Each candle represents a separate category of those lost. There are candles for police officers, firefighters, nurses, parents, children, siblings, and others. Volunteers are selected to come up and light these candles. Steve Spillman, one of John's close SJPD friends, comes up and lights the police officer candle, intoning, "Officer John Cahill, badge number 3357." Steve comes back to his chair directly behind me. As he sits down he squeezes my shoulders.

Then everyone in the room is asked to come up, light a candle, and announce the name of their loved one. I get up and Donna comes with me, holding my hand. I light the candle and speak into the microphone, "John Francis Cahill." I start back to my chair, trying to breathe, Donna holding my hand tighter. Toward the end a nine-year-old boy comes up with his mother, lights a candle, and in a shaky voice calls out his father's name. Then he says, "I'm going to take this candle home, and whenever I miss my dad I'll light it." Sitting here in this gathering of survivors, this collective attempt to cope, Donna and I look at each other. We're not alone.

As we leave we pick up a candle to take with us. Mine is a deep, almost navy blue—the same color as John's uniform. I bring it home and put it on my nightstand. It's still there.

* * *

In the spring of 2010 I return to the Jesuit Retreat Center for a weekend retreat and meet with my friend Father Bernie Bush, the same priest who helped me last year. This time I'm not here for the peaceful surroundings. I'm here for answers. As I walk into Bernie's office he gives me a hug and then notices the look on my face. "I can't tell if you're angry or depressed," he says.

"Sometimes I can't tell myself," I say. I bring him up to date and tell him that while I've heard John's voice speaking to me a number of times, and once I even heard God's voice, I'm still angry at times, not completely believing, not completely trusting.

He smiles and says, "What makes you think you're the only one?" Then he tells me, "You don't have a problem with faith, and you don't have a problem with trusting God. You have a problem with mystery." He looks at me. "You won't know everything and you won't understand everything until you're in the next life with God and with John." He assures me that in the meantime I'm on the right track by trying to live my life in honor of John, with love for my family and with trust in God, no matter how shaky that trust is.

A few days later when Donna and I read morning prayers, once again we come to Psalm 31: " . . . you are my rock and my refuge . . . " That gives me some comfort, but Bernie's right. I do have a problem with mystery. And I'll always have a problem with pain and loss.

But I don't have a problem with wanting to know everything about John's death. I still feel like I don't have all the answers about what happened. I'll probably never have all the answers—at least not answers to the important questions like how he lost his way so completely and I failed to see that—but I decide to request a copy of the Santa Cruz County Sheriff's report and the Coroner's report on John's death. A few days later the reports arrive in the mail in a single envelope. I leave the envelope, unopened, on my desk for a few days. I look at it, not sure if I really want to know its contents. But one morning, sitting at my desk, I realize that I do want to know everything I can about how my son died. I open the envelope and begin to read.

The Sheriff's report describes John as "lying supine" on the trail—meaning he was lying on his back, face up. The hiker who found John's body at 9:45 a.m. on the morning of December 4 couldn't tell if John was injured or dead, because he didn't get that close. The report states that the only vehicle in the parking lot at Henry Cowell State Park was John's blue-gray Honda pickup truck. John was "clad in hiking shoes, denim pants and a tan work jacket." That was his favorite jacket. "There was a black watch band and watch on the decedent's outstretched left hand." I wear that watch now, every day.

The report describes the .40 caliber Glock handgun found three feet from John's right side and says the gun was registered to John. The Glock was his backup; he'd given his regular off-duty weapon to Bruce the month before. Now I wonder whether, when John gave his gun to Bruce, he did it in good faith, checking it off as an item on his "right things to do" list—or if he was thinking he had another weapon if he needed it, or both.

The coroner's report describes John: "The body is 73 inches in length and weighs 192 pounds. The scalp hair is dark brown with gray and measures ¼ inch in length. The eyes are brown. There is a one-inch well-trimmed mustache." I pause and look at the picture on my bookshelf of the two of us taken on our last night together. I can't see any gray hair, and I don't remember any gray hair.

The report states that the entry wound was in front of his right ear and the exit wound was behind his left ear. The cartridge case was recovered but not the bullet.

I ask myself why I'm going over all this, why I requested these reports. Why do I need to know the details, why am I making myself relive the pain? The best answer I can come up with is that this was how John chose to die, and I feel like I should know about it. I also want to confirm what I have long suspected—that even with all his pain and despair, John was thoughtful enough not to disfigure his face; when I saw his body before he was embalmed, the back of his head was wrapped in a towel, but his face looked fine. But the most compelling reason for my scrutiny of these documents is that in spite of the pain of reliving of that time, I find some comfort, some connection with him, in knowing the details. I know this is an old-life connection and not a new-life connection, but I don't care. I'm his father. I want to know everything.

* * *

A day later I'm running errands, and I see a police officer get off his motorcycle and take off his helmet. He's wearing sunglasses. He's in his forties and six feet tall, with short, receding brown hair and a brown mustache. He walks into the local Starbucks. I keep looking at him. He isn't John. But he could be.

A few mornings later Donna reads morning prayers and Psalm 27: ". . . on a rock he sets me safe . . . " I spend the morning reflecting on the pain and loss that is still very much part of my existence, and at the same time, just as my priest friend Bernie Bush predicted, on the graces I've received in the last two years: the times I heard John's voice; Donna's love and support; the moment when I heard—experienced—God's voice last year; the constant reminders of God as my rock.

* * *

On the night of December 15, 2010, I'm lying in bed when suddenly I have the strongest disbelief attack I've had in a long time. I have one or two seconds of certainty that John can't be gone, followed by the familiar crunch of horror, the realization that he *is* gone, the memory of the day I found out, the memory of not being able to breathe when I was out on John's deck after they told me he was gone, after they told me they found his body on that mountain trail, after they told me he had put a bullet in his head. An hour later I manage to settle down and fall asleep. I have a long dream about John. Unlike most of my dreams, I remember this one when I wake up.

In the dream I'm in San Quentin—not as a volunteer, but as an inmate in blue jeans and blue denim shirt. I'm in a work party, and the guard who's supervising me is an unfriendly bureaucratic type who in real life used to be at the sally port when I came in on Tuesday nights. In the dream he has me moving heavy boxes, and he's forcing me to wear rectangular wooden paddles attached to my arms with rubber straps. I'm not able to use my hands or my fingers. It's very awkward lifting the boxes, and I'm boiling with frustration because I can't do the work.

The guard has me move a large, heavy box to another building using the paddles. As I approach the building, I see John standing outside. He doesn't see me. He's talking to Michele and they're discussing Kaitlin. They're conversing in the mildly friendly, civilized way that divorced couples use to keep the peace. Then I wake up.

When I share the dream with Donna, she says the paddles may represent my lack of control over John's death and everything that has happened since, and that John in the dream represents the fact that he's still working on behalf of Kaitlin. Donna also thinks the dream is another reminder that I couldn't stop John from doing what he did, that I wasn't in control. But I'm a slow learner, and I still don't really hear this when she says it, even after having that dream. I'm John's father, I think. I was supposed to stop him.

One morning before Christmas, Donna's walking past John's picture in my study—the picture of him standing in front of his motorcycle, thumbs hooked to his leather cartridge belt, a confident open-mouthed grin on his face. She looks at him and says aloud, "Take care of your dad and the girls."

Then she hears John speak, the same way I've heard John. This will be the first and last time Donna hears John say something. "I am," she hears.

"I know you are," Donna says to him silently. "Thank you." She starts to walk away, then turns back and says, "What if I'm still a little angry?"

"I know you are," John says. "But I still love you."

12

A Step Toward Healing

IT'S MARCH 28, 2011, and Donna and I are in the office of Dr. Adina Shore, waiting to see our granddaughter for the first time in two years. I'm praying that the connection Kaitlin's always had with Donna isn't broken. I'm also wondering how Kaitlin will relate to me, given what's been going on between Michele and me.

We haven't seen Kaitlin since March of 2009, and the Christmas card and gift we sent to her that year was returned by Michele unopened. In October of 2010 Dr. Shore had contacted Donna and me. Dr. Shore had been seeing Kaitlin on and off since John died. and she told us she felt strongly that Kaitlin needed us back in her life. A couple of months later Donna and I met with Dr. Shore. She was clearly dedicated to Kaitlin and committed to getting us together with her, but she made it clear that I had to deal with my anger toward Michele and move toward forgiveness because that would be best for Kaitlin. Part of me knew she was right, and Donna had been trying to convince me that holding onto my anger helped no one and was toxic for me. But, ever the slow learner, I secretly thought that the most I'd be able to do was get to the point of being respectful and civilized with Michele when we were picking up and dropping off our granddaughter.

One night during that time I dreamed that Donna and I were standing by a river in a small city. On the other side were a series of booths for an arts and crafts show. We could see Kaitlin standing over there, and Donna wanted to go to her. I felt that we should be careful since we didn't have Michele's approval, but Donna insisted we should go to Kaitlin. We had to go down our side of the bank until we could cross the river on a bridge, then we had to come back up to where the booths were located. I lost sight of Donna and proceeded to climb a series of wooden stairs. Each set of steps was a dead end, and I had to turn around and come back down. I never found Donna or Kaitlin. I woke up and lay there thinking about the dream. I decided the point was that I'd never get reconnected to Kaitlin without heeding Donna's advice about my anger.

On a Tuesday night not long after my dream, at the spirituality group in San Quentin, the topic was how we respond to God's call. After all the men spoke I told them that I knew God was calling me to let my anger go and forgive Michele, but I was struggling with that. At the end of the session, Clint, who's been in prison for over thirty years, came over and showed me a passage in the footnote to the Psalms, saying it might help me. The theme of the passage was trust in God because anger and worry are fruitless. Clint put his arm around me and said, "You have to let this go, for you and for your granddaughter. Put it in God's hands."

Clint is three inches taller than I am. I looked up into his face and said, "I'll try, but I'm really struggling with this."

He looked down at me. "Try harder," he whispered softly but firmly.

* * *

A few days later, on the second anniversary of John's death, Donna and I hiked the Golden Gate Trail. On Dr. Shore's suggestion I threw a stone in the water, representing the release of my anger at Michele. I knew I'd probably have to throw more than one stone, but it was a start. Between late January and late March Donna and I met three more times with Kaitlin's therapist to continue working on what it would take for us to be able to see Kaitlin. In effect, Dr. Shore was serving as a mediator between us and Michele, trying to establish mutually accepted conditions that would allow Kaitlin to visit us and resume a relationship with us. I was still angry with Michele, but Donna and Adina kept reminding me that the only issue here was Kaitlin's best interest, and that the best way to honor John was for us to have a relationship with Kaitlin, which meant reaching real peace with Michele.

Now I'm nervous as we wait for Kaitlin to join us in Dr. Shore's office. Michele is dropping her off and will come back and pick her up later. As I sit here in a chair next to Donna in Dr. Shore's waiting room, I wonder how much damage has been done to our relationship with Kaitlin during the two years without any contact. Finally she comes through the door. She has the same blue eyes and long, light brown hair, but she's three inches taller than the last time we saw her, and I realize she's no longer a little girl. She spots Donna. With a slight smile of relief, she slowly glides into Donna's arms. "Hi Grandma," she says, and they stand there holding on to each other. I feel tense, bracing myself for the possibility of getting a different greeting. Then, beautiful fourteen-year-old Kaitlin, who's two inches taller than her grandma, looks over Donna's shoulder at me, disengages from Donna, and walks into my arms. Neither of us says anything, but now I know that I haven't lost my granddaughter.

We spend the time giving Kaitlin gifts and catching up with each other's lives. Donna and I follow Kaitlin's lead and make no reference to John. The time flies by, but it's clear that Kaitlin wants us in her life and wants to be in ours. After Kaitlin leaves, Donna and I walk out of the office, feeling grateful to Adina, our feet not touching the ground.

In July we see Kaitlin a second time. This time we have a long lunch with her and then walk through the shops in Capitola, near Santa Cruz. Donna buys Kaitlin a dress. Kaitlin talks about future visits and coming to our house to spend time with us. We're in a bakery when it's time for her to go; Michele is in her car outside waiting for her. Kaitlin hugs and kisses me and does the same with Donna. She starts to walk out the door, then turns around and comes back to me. She puts her head on my chest, holds onto me, and tells me she loves me. I stand there, holding my granddaughter, knowing with total certainty that not only is our love for each other unbroken, but in that moment she's seeking the part of me that's her dad, and I'm seeking the part of her dad that lives in her.

Donna and I have a third great visit with Kaitlin. This time she's excited about starting her freshman year of high school. She's also a cheerleader. I'm wondering what happened to the five-year-old who used to like to collect bugs with me.

During August and early September, Dr. Shore continues working with Donna and me, and separately with Michele, to move us to reconciliation—which, she keeps reminding us all, is in Kaitlin's best interest. She's working with Michele on her issues of pain and anger; she's working with me; Donna is helping her work with me on my own issues of pain and anger. While I'm trying to move toward forgiveness, I'm still thinking that the important thing is to get to a place where Michele and I can be respectful and civil toward each other when Donna and I pick up Kaitlin and drop her off. I think that this might be the most I'm capable of doing, forgiveness-wise.

Finally, Adina has us all agreeing to meet. The day arrives and we walk into Adina's office. I go first. I don't know what to expect. Michele is sitting there on the couch, rigid. Without thinking, without knowing I'm going to do it, I hold out my arms and Michele stands and comes right into them. We hold onto each other, crying. Michele keeps saying, "I'm sorry, I'm so sorry."

I tell her, "I'm sorry too." We're standing there, sobbing, leaning on each other, and, without using the word, forgiving each other.

Finally Donna says, "Hey, I want a hug too." Michele hugs Donna and tells her how much she's missed her. They stand there together, crying. For the moment Adina's not the therapist but the Kleenex supplier.

When we finally stop crying and sit down, I tell Michele that we've all had enough pain to last a lifetime. I tell her that I'll always respect the fact that she's Kaitlin's mother, and that I want us all to be done with the anger and pain that drove us apart. Michele tells us how bad she feels about what happened and about what she did. Later during this visit she tells us how unsupported and condemned she felt in the aftermath of John's death. Listening to her, I begin to see her perspective and what it must have been like for her.

We talk about our next visit with Kaitlin, our plans for Kaitlin's birthday, and other things we'll do together. I tell Michele that she didn't put the gun to John's head, that he made his own choice. For the first time I'm able to separate my anger toward Michele from my anguish at losing John. I begin to realize that I've been carrying this dead weight of anger every day for the last two and a half years, stupidly wasting energy that could have gone to life-affirming steps rather than hateful feelings. I feel the anger leaving my body. The anguish over John's death isn't going anywhere, but the weight isn't as heavy.

Michele and I tell each other "I'm sorry" at least a half dozen more times. In *Psychology Today*, Beverly Engel, an author and psychotherapist, has said, "Apology is an important ritual, a way of showing respect for the wronged person. Apology has the ability to disarm others of their anger and to prevent further misunderstandings. While an apology cannot undo harmful past actions, if done sincerely and effectively, it can undo the negative effects of those actions."

We all part with more hugging and more tears, and with the realization that this is not only good for Kaitlin, it's good for us—a relief for all of us, a lighter load for all of us. After Michele drives away Donna and I stand in the parking lot. I'm completely amazed, having never expected such a grace-filled reconciliation.

As we're driving home Donna receives a text message from Michele: "I feel a heavy weight lifted. Anger is a burden. I'm so happy. I don't ever want us to be separate again."

In *Traveling Mercies*, Anne Lamott writes, "I do not at all understand the mystery of grace—only that it meets us where we are, but does not leave us where it found us."

* * *

A few days later Donna and I drive down to Malibu Grand Prix, in Red-wood City, a miniature racecar track where we used to take Kaitlin, and, much earlier, Danielle. Kaitlin has asked to come here for our next out-ing. We meet Adina Shore, Kaitlin, and Michele. Kaitlin gives us big hugs and presents us with a homemade birthday card made out to both Donna and me for our September birthdays. In it she's written how much she loves spending time with us and that she can't wait to come and visit us in San Francisco. She also tells us she can't wait to do more "fashion shows"—when she was young she used to dress me up in an assortment of old dresses and scarves and slather me with makeup. I've been sort of hoping we might be done with this activity, but I realize that even at fourteen there's still some little girl in Kaitlin, and if I have to wear makeup I will.

We have lunch and then Adina leaves and Kaitlin rides the racecars. I sit there watching her, filled with happiness and gratitude that our grand-daughter is back in our life. Then I remember that the last time Kaitlin and I were here John was with us. It was a Saturday in late October, six weeks be-fore he died. It was after he had gotten depressed and started having anxiety attacks but before he had suicidal thoughts. He and I watched Kaitlin race around the track and waved at her as she came by us. But our focus that day was not on Kaitlin enjoying herself. It was on her father's depression and, for me, on problem-solving: trying to get John to focus on the positive aspects of his life, on repeatedly affirming that he would come out of this, and still not having a clue that he wouldn't come out of this, that I couldn't help him come out of it.

Sitting here now, watching Kaitlin speeding around the racetrack as Donna and Michele stand down by the fence cheering her on, I know that being reconciled with Michele and reunited with Kaitlin is a gift of grace, but that grace does not offset the loss of my son. It doesn't soften the pain of John's death. It doesn't blunt the reality of what he did.

Later, at Adina's suggestion, Donna, Michele, Kaitlin and I go to a nearby picnic area, tear up printouts of all the angry e-mails Michele and I have sent each other, place them in a barbeque pit with some small cedar branches Adina gave us, and burn them. I don't know if Kaitlin has read any of these e-mails, but I know from Adina that Kaitlin has been feeling the tension between her mom and us. And earlier today, when Michele and I greeted each other with a long hug, I could see a look of relief and happiness on Kaitlin's face.

As the papers burn I pray aloud, "May the spirit of family, the spirit of forgiveness, the spirit of love always win out." Michele prays, "We will always honor John as a good man, as Brian's son, as Kaitlin's father, and as my first husband." Donna adds, "No one is perfect, and if something creeps up and bothers us, I pray that we can continue to talk about it and then forgive and forget." Kaitlin is standing between Michele and me. She doesn't say anything, but before the prayers she put her left hand on her mom's shoulder and her right hand on my shoulder, and she keeps her hands there until we finish praying.

Afterward Michele and Kaitlin and Donna and I have dinner together in a nearby restaurant, and, for the first time in a long while, experience the joy of family in each other's company.

At the end of the night Michele suggests I meet her in the school parking lot tomorrow night; Kaitlin's cheerleading at the freshman football game, and Michele thinks it would be fun to surprise her by coming into the stadium together.

That night in the shower, I tell John that we got to see his daughter today, and I tell him how beautiful she is. I tell him how much she wants to be part of our lives and how much she wants us to be part of hers. Then I realize John already knows all that.

Donna's at work the next afternoon so I drive alone to Hollister where Michele and Kaitlin are living with Michele's new husband, Dave. As I head south on Highway 101 beyond San Jose, I see the sign for Parkway Lake, a trout pond where John took Kaitlin to catch her first trout. When John called and told me about it, I reminded him that his grandfather would be very proud that he was keeping the Cahill trout fishing tradition alive.

I meet Michele and we walk into the stadium together. Kaitlin's on the field, doing some pre-game practicing with her cheerleading group. She spots us and breaks out in a big, surprised smile. Michele and I sit in the stands, both of us still marveling at our reconciliation. We agree that our burning ceremony was powerful and that we appreciate the fact that we're sitting there together, not hating each other, enjoying each other's company, watching Kaitlin—connected with each other, if we're honest, by Kaitlin.

Anne Lamott writes: "Families are definitely the training ground for forgiveness. At some point you pardon the people in your family for being stuck together in all their weirdness, and when you can do that, you can learn to pardon anyone."

Two years ago, when our conflicts with Michele escalated, Krissy had understandably sided with her mom and pulled away from Donna and me. But between Christmas and New Year's of this year, when Kaitlin is visiting us, Krissy calls and asks if she can come up too. Donna makes it clear how much we want her to be with us and how much we love her and have missed her, and the next morning, just as we're finishing breakfast, Krissy pulls up in front of the house. I don't want to wait, so I rush down the front steps and am standing on the sidewalk behind her car when she gets out. She turns and spots me and comes into my arms. "I've always loved you and I always will," I say.

"I know," she says softly, and we stand there crying. Donna, wondering what the delay is, comes down the front steps. Krissy looks over my shoulder, sees her grandmother, and goes to her. More tears, more expressions of love, more holding on. Donna and I smile at each other. Both our granddaughters are back in our life.

13

Cops and Cons

IT'S A JULY DAY in 2011, eighteen months after I told Janet I wanted to get involved in suicide prevention for cops, and I'm sitting in a classroom at the San Francisco Police Academy waiting to be introduced. I'm here to talk to twenty-five veteran SF cops about my son's suicide. Since I told Janet I would like to help other cops, I've written an opinion piece in the *San Francisco Chronicle* about cops and suicide, and that resulted in a meeting between me and Sergeant Mary Dunnigan, who heads the SFPD behavioral science unit. Mary has invited me here to tell John's story, to summarize what's in the literature about cops and suicide, and to tell my audience of cops that if this can happen to John Cahill, it can happen to any cop.

I look at the officers in the classroom, a third of them women, all of them in uniform. They are here because they're required to do forty hours of training every two years. Most of that training relates to officer safety, tactics, and weapons, but two hours of it relates to self-care, and that's what Mary is in charge of. I notice that two or three cops are dozing off. A number are consulting their cell phones. Most are giving the clear impression that they don't want to be here.

Mary begins to introduce me and I suddenly realize that while I really wanted to do this, to tell John's story to help cops, now I'm not so sure. I wipe my sweaty palms on my Dockers, starting to get that familiar feeling of not being able to breathe. Mary finishes her introduction and turns to me. I wipe my hands one more time, take a half-breath, and start speaking.

"My grandfather was a San Francisco firefighter and my uncle was a San Francisco police officer. But I'm not a cop. I'm the father of a cop who took his life on December 3, 2008. He was forty-two years old. He was a police officer for nineteen years." All of a sudden, the cell phones are put away.

A few officers are elbowing their colleagues to wake them up. Everyone is sitting up, listening.

I'm breathing better, and after I tell them what I'm going to talk about, I say that if suicide can happen to John Cahill, it can happen to any cop anywhere. I pause and say, "And you should know that, because you lost three of your own last year." A number of officers nod their heads. One young cop has a stricken look on his face. I find out later that he was close to one of the officers who committed suicide in 2010.

I tell these officers about John Francis Cahill: son, husband, father, cop, backpacker, and scuba diver—a vibrant man, healthy and full of life—until the last year and half of his life. I tell them about John's divorce and what led up to his suicide, about how even at the end I thought he was doing all the right things: seeing a counselor, talking with me, trying to focus on the positives in his life, especially his daughters. More nods. I'm pretty sure I can tell which cops are parents.

I tell them how I learned about John's suicide and admit that I never saw it coming, that my perception of John as healthy and strong never allowed me to think he could do this. I say that I thought that just as I had come through a painful divorce, John would come through his. More nods, and I think I can tell which cops have been through a divorce.

I look out at the group. "I want to try to briefly summarize recent research on law enforcement and suicide. This is not what I planned to be doing in my retirement, and I'm not a cop or a researcher, just a father of a cop who lost his way. But I think you need to know this." There is dead silence in the classroom. Some officers are looking down. I can see a couple of officers fighting back tears. Some are still not reacting in any way.

I begin to tell my audience what I've learned about cops and suicide, from my reading and my talks with my counselor, Janet Childs. I start by saying that the research shows that a good cop is highly functioning in all aspects of his or her life. A good cop is trained to bring control out of chaos. A good cop is willing to risk everything in the critical incident. These characteristics and habits are useful for cops, but they can become lethal when a cop has a personal problem and becomes seriously depressed. The critical incidents cops deal with in their jobs are finite and usually come quickly to an end, but the critical incidents cops deal with in their personal lives—divorce, financial ruin, and so forth—often drag on and on. When they do, the cop gets depressed. Depression erodes the cop's sense of self-worth; the cop gets frustrated because he can't control the situation, and he comes to believe that the pain—his (or her) own "critical incident"—will never end. This feeling globalizes into how he feels about everything in his life.

I tell the group that as John got more depressed after his divorce, he started to believe he wasn't being a good cop. I remember him telling me three months before his death, "I'm not any good at work." At the time I told him that if that were true, one of his supervisors would have talked to him about it. And when John was worrying about the impact of the divorce on Kaitlin, he began to question whether he was a good father. Donna and I both told him that he was being a great father, getting Kaitlin into counseling at the time of the divorce, encouraging Kaitlin to express her feelings, and making sure that Kaitlin knew that she did not cause the divorce and that both her parents would always love her. But now I know that John couldn't hear what we were saying.

Around that time John told me that for the first time in his life, he couldn't control things. One day on the phone he said, "I've never not been in control before, and I can't stand it." And as his depression continued with no end in sight, he began to despair, to believe that the situation, the painful factors around his divorce, his sense of failure and shame—his "critical incident"—would never end. In early November he told me on the phone, "This is never going to end." I reassured him that it would end, that he would come out the other end and still have a good life. But he didn't hear me— that's what I think now, what I know now, because of what I know about cops and suicide, about suicide in general.

I explain to the officers that back then I didn't understand that John's role and identity as a cop were significant factors in what happened to him. But even as I say that—even though I've told the officers about John thinking he was functioning poorly, that John was frustrated by his lack of control and despairing that the situation would never end—I find myself wondering how much these theories really did apply to John. Did he take his life because he was a cop? If he hadn't been a cop, would he have still taken his life? In that moment, facing these officers, I can't answer these questions.

I continue my presentation and tell the group that John was wrong, of course, about his perceived lack of value as a cop and a parent, but these perceptions were his version of reality during the last stage of his life. And I couldn't change his perceptions, because by then he couldn't hear me.

I tell the officers about sitting on my deck with John a few days before he took his life. He was calm—still depressed, but calm. I say that now I know he may have already decided to end his life. According to the research, after an individual decides to end their life, they regain a sense of control and calmness. Usually they act on their decision within a few days. I believe John delayed acting on his decision until after my retirement dinner.

I reference Ellen Kirschman, author of *I Love a Cop,* on how the physical and emotional stress of a cop's job changes the individual. Kirschman maintains that cops are oriented toward control and can have a distorted but culturally correct sense of invincibility and independence. "From the beginning, cops are taught to maintain an occupational persona: a 'public face' that makes them always appear to be in control, on top of things, knowledgeable and unafraid. A cop's distress can result from a tangled series of events, often including a devastating relationship loss, and [creating] a temporarily hopeless outlook." That was John.

I tell them about Kevin Gilmartin, a former police officer who wrote *Emotional Survival for Law Enforcement.* He writes, "Although in many ways officers are winning the battle of street survival, they appear to be fatally losing the battle of emotional survival." I try to hammer home Gilmartin's main message: The very things that make you a good cop—safe and effective on the street—can screw up your personal life and, in some cases, destroy you.

A few months later, at a training conference in San Francisco, I will meet Kevin Gilmartin. Mary Dunnigan, the head of the unit, introduced me to him after his talk. I knew I only had a few minutes to speak to him, and I found myself telling him about John. I told him about John's background, his life as a cop, and his divorce. I told him that I didn't think John had post-traumatic stress disorder like many cops do. He looked at me with sad eyes and said, "It doesn't matter. Being a cop for nineteen years was a factor in his death." I thanked him and walked away, asking myself once again the question I've been asking myself during this first training: Would John have done this if he hadn't been a cop? I still had no answer, but in my head I heard what Gilmartin had just said to me, "Being a cop was a factor in his death." And then I heard Gilmartin say, "It doesn't matter." It doesn't matter whether John had PTSD. And then I remembered once again, as I have to keep remembering over and over, it really doesn't matter—because John's gone. I can't bring him back.

Was being a cop what caused him to do what he did? What I think now, as I write this, is that being a cop *was* a factor, but it wasn't the only factor. John had no experience with pain and failure before his divorce; he was a strong, confident, happy young man and remained strong, happy and confident until the last eighteen months of life. His sense of failure and shame about the divorce and all the related issues changed all that and was a huge factor in him doing what he did. It was really that, combined with the fact that he was a cop and everything that went with it, that probably pushed him over the edge.

As I come to the end of my presentation, I tell the officers that the research of Thomas Joiner, author of *Myths about Suicide,* shows that in most cases suicide is not an act of cowardice and that the individual who commits suicide often has a strong personality. I can tell by the looks on many faces that this is a new concept for cops. Joiner believes that individuals who commit suicide become convinced they're a burden, that they don't belong, and their loved ones will be better without them. I tell the group that I believe John thought his daughters would be better off without him. He was as wrong as he could be, but that was his reality in the last stage of his life. I look out again at the group of officers and all I see is sadness.

Finally, I tell the officers that the *Badge of Life,* a national organization of former police officers dedicated to preventing law enforcement suicide, reports that 150 cops take their own lives every year. The *Badge of Life* also reports that for every police officer that commits suicide, there are a thousand officers dealing with post-traumatic stress disorder and another thousand cops struggling with marital issues, depression, or alcoholism. I remind them that police suicide happens at a far greater rate than police homicide or duty-related accidental deaths. That makes a few officers look up.

I tell them that as a result of John's suicide, San Jose PD has changed their approach: They've developed an agency-wide mandatory training program and told their officers that they should come in if they're depressed; their situation will be kept confidential, they'll receive counseling, and they won't lose their jobs. In the year after John died, twelve cops came in, got confidential help, and stayed on the job. I remind the officers that asking for help is a sign of strength, not a sign of weakness. I tell them that just as they are aware of the obvious risks in their work, they also have to be aware of the hidden risks: depression, substance abuse, divorce, and in some cases—in the case of John Cahill—suicide.

When I'm done there's dead silence, no applause. No one knows what to say. Finally, Mary Dunnigan tells the class they have a ten-minute break before their next session. Some officers get up, walk by me, and don't say anything. They can't wait to get out of there. I know they were paying attention, but they're probably not comfortable with the topic or know what to say to me. A number of officers do come up and thank me. I'm shaking their hands, looking at them, wishing one of them was John. Then I realize that if John were here I wouldn't be here. I wouldn't be doing this. I wouldn't be spending my retirement learning about cops and suicide. I wouldn't be telling them about my son's suicide. I wouldn't be telling cops about the hidden risks of their work. I would gladly give up this experience and go back to the time when I was blissfully ignorant about cops and suicide. But I know I can't go back. And I feel that I can do some good. I feel like I can help some cops. I feel like I can honor my son.

Mary thanks me and tells me she'd like me to do this training on a weekly basis if I'm willing. I tell her yes, but as I'm standing there I feel the urge to bolt from the room without knowing why. I say goodbye and head out of the building. I get to my car, open the door and get in. I'm crying before I can close the door, and it comes to me full force that I haven't just done some academic presentation about suicide; I've told the story of my son's suicide. Before I know it I'm having trouble breathing; I'm back on the deck at John's condo, back with the disbelief, shock, horror. I sit in my car, finally realizing what Janet has been trying to tell me. I can do this. I can help cops. I can honor my son. But there will be a price.

A week later I do a second SFPD training session. Afterward a number of the officers come up and thank me. While I'm talking to them I notice a cop about John's age and build standing in the back of the classroom, waiting until the other officers are through talking to me. Finally he comes up to me and asks, "Can we talk outside?" We go out to the parking lot, and I see there are tears in his eyes. He tells me, "You just told my story, only I'm not dead yet." He describes his situation, which is very similar to John's.

I start to tell him all the things I tried to tell John, but I suddenly realize that none of that did any good. Instead I look him in the eye, grab both of his shoulders, and say, "If there was only one thing that I could go back and tell my son, it would be how wrong he was to think that his daughters would be better off without him." I'm still holding onto his shoulders, and we're both crying. "And you would be so wrong to ever consider, even in your darkest time," I add, "that your children would be better off without you." He thanks me, wipes his eyes and heads back in for his next training session.

* * *

On the first Tuesday of October, after I've done a dozen or so SFPD training sessions, I walk into the police academy classroom and realize I've gotten slightly more comfortable making this presentation every week. And I've learned some things. I've especially learned not to look back at the pictures of John that are on the screen as I'm talking.

Today I'm struck by the fact that the great majority of the officers in this group are in their late forties and early fifties—usually I get a mix of people in their twenties, thirties, and forties, with maybe one or two in their fifties. As I start speaking I realize that, unlike the people in the other SFPD groups I've addressed, these men and women are all intensely focusing on what I'm saying, all responsive and nodding. It dawns on me that these officers have been around long enough to understand the emotional price of police work and the hidden risks of their jobs. Most of them come up and thank me afterwards. They tell me how valuable it was for them to hear what I had to say, how valuable it would be for all cops to hear it, and how much they respect me for talking about it. A tall, gray-haired Irish sergeant gives me his card and says, "You're providing a real service for us. If I can ever do anything for you let me know."

As I'm leaving, Mary Dunnigan, the SFPD sergeant in charge of the training, tells me that the evaluations for my first three months of presentations are very positive. I'm glad to be doing this. I know there's a price to pay, but I'm clear that I'm supposed to be doing this, clear that I'm supposed to be honoring my son this way.

* * *

I get back in my car and head over to San Quentin for the Tuesday evening spirituality group. I've been co-leading this inmate session since early 2010. Now, for the first time since I started working with the police department, it dawns on me that I must be the only person in the world who spends Tuesday afternoons with a bunch of cops and Tuesday evenings with a bunch of convicts—my day with cops and cons. I'm still smiling about this when I spot the massive tan cellblocks of San Quentin. Cops and cons: I've got both ends of the criminal justice system covered.

That night in the spirituality group one of the men reads from Chapter 23 of Mathew's Gospel in the Bible, where Jesus is challenging the Pharisees: "You have neglected the weightier matters of the law—justice, mercy and faith." There's a lively discussion about what's more important: justice, mercy, or faith. Finally one of the guys says, "Let's face it—if we don't have faith we're screwed; if we don't show mercy we're not following Jesus; and if we forget about justice then we're not owning up to what we did that got us here." I sit there looking at these guys, thinking that the cops I was with this afternoon might be pleasantly surprised if they were sitting with us here tonight.

A few days later it's a Sunday evening and I'm standing behind a long serving table with six other volunteers, just below the altar in the San Quentin chapel. I'm wearing an apron and latex gloves, leaning over a large tray of sliced roast beef. It's hot in here and I'm trying not to drip sweat into the serving tray, but I have to keep moving. I have a long line of hungry men anxiously waiting to fill their plates. The volunteer on my right is serving scalloped potatoes and the colleague on my left is serving mixed vegetables. Other volunteers serve green salad, rolls and butter, and orange Kool-Aid; later on another volunteer will serve ice cream.

We're at San Quentin's yearly banquet for the men who regularly attend Sunday Mass or are involved in various chapel study groups, classes, and interfaith discussions. The dinner is also intended to attract men who may have been away from church for some time. The food is donated by a local restaurant, prepared by students at a local university, and brought in and served by those of us who volunteer in the chapel. The guys know that there's always great food on this night, so usually 250 men sign up for the event. Jesuit Father George Williams, our new chaplain, is supervising the event this evening. He previously worked in the Massachusetts prison system, and it's already obvious he has a great touch with the men.

Tonight, after the guys have finished eating and we're beginning to clean up, a large, tough-looking, fifty-year-old Hispanic inmate comes up to me. He has a serious look on his face. At first he doesn't say anything, and I'm not sure what to do. Then he reaches out his hand and says quietly, "Thank you." He gives my hand a long, bone-crushing shake. Then he looks down at his feet.

"I'm Brian," I say. "What's your name?"

He glances at me and says, "I'm Francisco." He looks down again and I realize he's trying not to cry. "I've been in and out of prison all my life, and I've never had an experience like this," he explains in a low voice. "I'm not just talking about the good food, but all you guys from the outside, serving us, caring for us. I've never felt that kind of love before."

I don't know what to say, so I invite him to come to Mass next Sunday.

"I haven't been to church for a long time," he says.

I smile and say, "That's not a problem. If you want, come on by and maybe I'll see you there." He nods but doesn't say anything.

A few weeks later when I come in for Mass, I see Francisco sitting alone in the third pew from the front on the right side. I walk up the aisle and sit next to him. This time I'm prepared for the bone-crushing handshake. After Mass we sit and talk in the pew after everyone else has left. He tells me this is his fourth time down. I ask him if he wants this to be his last time in prison. He looks at me and says, "Yeah, but this is all I know. I've been in the drug business all my life. My family is in the business. This last time I got caught driving a load over the border. This is what I do."

I sit there, realizing that I'm completely out of my league. "Francisco, all I know is that you're in this chapel for a reason. I also know that God loves you and wants to lead you."

"Well," he says, "I would like to get out of here and stay out so I can be with my daughter. Do you think God would help me with that?"

I look at him and say, "I know He would."

After that day, Francisco starts coming to Mass every Sunday, and eventually he joins our Tuesday night spirituality group. He says nothing during the first few weeks, but I can see he's listening intently when the other men express their feelings, talk about their pasts, and describe feeling

God's love. Then one night when it's his turn to share, he looks around the room and says haltingly, "Listening to some of you these last few weeks, I'm beginning to see that maybe God can love me in spite of what I've done. And maybe I can change the way I've lived my life, and maybe I don't have to do the stuff I've done to survive." Then he's silent again and sits looking down at his lap, as though he feels exhausted by this effort to express himself. A number of the guys in the group thank him, and the men on either side of him pat him on the back.

A few weeks later the guys in the spirituality group are sharing stories about how they got in there and what's happened to them since. Tony, who's been in prison for thirty years, talks about his violent, hateful outlook in the early years of his confinement, the resulting time that he spent in isolation cells, and finally, his discovery that he was his own worst enemy. He's a leader, a teacher in the San Quentin violence prevention program, and a man of faith respected by all the men in the group. He will be paroled in a year and go to work for a non-profit that provides reentry services for inmates getting out of state prison.

I notice Francisco watching Tony, listening intently. When it's Francisco's turn to speak, he looks at Tony and says, "I don't know how to change. I want to, for my daughter, but I don't know how. I only know life in here and life outside moving drugs."

Tony looks at him. "I only knew violence and hate in here and outside," he says. "But there's more. We can find it, but we need God's help. We need to pray. God is willing to help us." Tony pauses, swings around to face Francisco more fully, and says again, "God is ready and willing to help you."

Francisco looks at Tony and nods. Then he looks at me and nods.

About six weeks later I'm at the San Quentin chapel for Sunday Mass. I'm sitting in the left rear of the chapel with a young inmate I'm just coming to know. At the end of Mass I spot Francisco, sitting in his regular place up front on the right. He's broken his leg and hasn't been to the spirituality group for a while. He gets up from his pew. Even with a walking cast and using a cane, he's moving fast in my direction. He clearly has something to tell me. I realize this is the first time I'm not the one initiating contact between us.

As he comes closer, I see anger and frustration in his face. He tells me that he had a Father's Day visit with his mother and his teenage daughter, and the visit didn't go well. I ask him what happened, and he tells me his daughter has been getting F's in school. He chewed her out, telling her she was lazy and irresponsible and that she was hurting her future. His daughter got upset and refused to talk to him. His mother got upset and told him he was in no position to be judging his daughter or anyone else. They left before the visiting time was up.

Francisco looks at me and says, "I feel like I just want to stay here. I'm supposed to be getting out in less than a year, but I don't know. And if I do get out, it would be so easy to go back to what I know."

I put my hand on his shoulder. "I don't know much, but I know you're not supposed to stay in here, and when you are released, you're not supposed to go back to your old work." I ask him, "You love your daughter, right?"

He nods.

We sit down in one of the pews and I say, "I think part of what you're upset about is that you're in here and not in control of your daughter's life." I pause and give him a long look. "I know about not being in control. My oldest son took his life and I couldn't control that. I couldn't stop it. My daughter struggles with depression and is in and out of my life, and I can't control that. But I can do something. I can pray. I can pray for my children. I can try to be the best father I can." I pause again. "That's what you can do. You can pray. Everything starts with prayer. You can talk to your counselor about paroling to a halfway house. And you're an experienced truck driver. Maybe you can take that experience and put it to good use, turn it into something positive. And when you're out there, working, you can be your daughter's father, the father you want to be, the father she wants you to be."

Francisco nods. There's a little less anger and frustration in his face.

In two years he will be a free man, working as a truck driver, and enjoying a good relationship with his daughter.

14

Giving Thanks

MICHELE AND I MEET for lunch in San Jose. We're still feeling elated and grateful for our reconciliation. We talk about John's last few weeks. She isn't trying to deny his pain and depression about the divorce, the finances, and the house; but she says she's been haunted by the sense that John seemed to be moving on and looking forward to life after divorce, and then at some point he stopped being able to keep moving on.

Sitting there with Michele, I remember that Dr. Shore had the same impression. She had seen John on the day before he died, when he brought Kaitlin in for her counseling session, and according to her he showed no signs of serious depression. I tell Michele that I believe John was very depressed from August 2008 on, and his depression got worse in October and even worse in November. And as his depression worsened he began to feel he was a burden to his loved ones, and he made sure we didn't know, at the end, just how lost he truly was.

Driving home after lunch, I find myself going over those last few months once again, still seeing the signals I missed, still feeling I let him slip through my fingers, still feeling like I failed him.

A few days later, I wake up at five a.m. after a nightmare. In the dream I was hiking on a steep hillside in San Francisco. The hill was full of beautiful homes and looked out at the San Francisco Bay. As I was walking up a trail, a man, a woman, and a young teenage girl were standing on their lawn beside a house, near a steep cliff. The man and the woman were arguing. The man was very angry and seemed very controlling. The woman said, "I've had enough," and she stepped off the cliff. I kept climbing up the trail until I was on a wooden walkway in front of another house. There were people standing there, looking in the window of the house, and they were clearly upset.

I asked them what was wrong, and they told me that a young teenage girl in the house had just committed suicide.

I wake up and sit up in bed, feeling depressed, still in the world of the dream. In a few minutes the alarm goes off. Donna turns toward me, sees the look on my face, and asks, "What's wrong?" I tell her about the dream.

She thinks for a moment and then she reaches over and hugs me. "You've been focusing on suicide. Kaitlin is uppermost on your mind. Maybe you're unconsciously worried about her."

We get out of bed, kneel down and pray for our granddaughter, trying to put her in God's hands. Afterwards I tell Donna that I have been a bit worried that the literature suggests that children of parents who have committed suicide are also at risk of suicide.

Donna looks at me and says, "Then we'll have to pray harder, and we'll have to work harder to make sure that doesn't happen, and we'll have to love both our granddaughters intensely and make them feel that love all the time." Then she puts her hand on my shoulder and says, "But remember, we can't control their lives any more than you could control John's life, no matter how much you loved him."

On a Friday evening in late October, Donna and I pull into the parking lot at the football stadium at Kaitlin's high school. "I want to see Kaitlin before she starts cheerleading," Donna says, and she jumps out of the car and goes into the stadium while I search for a parking space. I come into the stadium after the game has started and climb up the steps to sit with Donna and Michele in the stands. Kaitlin's engrossed in her cheering so she doesn't notice me. At halftime I go down to the field. Kaitlin spots me, runs over, and jumps into my embrace, her arms wrapped around my shoulders, almost knocking me down. I stand there holding onto my granddaughter— the most intense moment of pure joy I've experienced since well before John died.

Shortly after that Michele calls to tell us that Kaitlin has been on the Internet and found the *San Francisco Chronicle* opinion piece I wrote about John and cops and suicide. In the article I stated that John was concerned about the impact of the divorce on his youngest daughter. Kaitlin's initial reaction was to think that she had somehow caused her dad's suicide, but Michele and Dr. Shore jumped on that and reassured her it wasn't the case. Michele also tells us that recently there was a school-wide discussion or seminar about suicide. For the first time Kaitlin was able to speak about her dad with her friends. Michele and I say goodbye, I hang up, and Donna looks at me and says, "If Kaitlin is able to talk about John and what happened, that's a very good sign."

Later I find myself wishing that Kaitlin didn't have to talk about her dad at school, didn't have to tell her friends what happened to him, that instead she could bring her dad to career day at school and have him talk about being a cop.

* * *

It's a mid-November Wednesday and I'm spending the day reading a book summarizing the most recent research on suicide. Donna has been visiting her parents in Pittsburgh; she'll fly home Sunday morning. I fix myself some soup for dinner and on the spur of the moment I decide to watch John's video. I find the CD, put it in the disk drive, and sit back in my recliner. Pretty soon I'm sitting there watching my son as an infant, a toddler, a teenager, a young adult, a young police officer. Suddenly I can't believe how fast he grew up, and I'm overwhelmed by a sense of being cheated, of being robbed, not just because of his death, his absence, but because it feels like his short life flew by me at blinding speed. That night in the shower I'm crying and I don't hear him. I haven't heard him in a long time. Over the next few days I sink a little lower, not just because Donna is away, not just because I feel so cheated by John's short life, but because this time three years ago John was living in a nightmare, and he wasn't going to get the chance to wake up.

On Friday night before I fix my dinner I pour myself a Jameson. Yes, this is November, the month before he died three years ago, and yes, I am buried in suicide and grief literature and writing and training, but I can't escape the fact that I'm learning, still learning, about death and loss and pain—the reality of it, the permanence of it, the pervasiveness of it—not just intellectually or even emotionally, but viscerally. I pour myself a second Jameson with the hope that numbness will catch up with depression. It doesn't.

On Sunday afternoon we're sitting at a round luncheon table in the main dining room of the Irish Cultural Center in San Francisco. Earlier I picked up Donna at the airport, and we came directly here to celebrate a baby christening. The mother is the daughter of Donna's best friend who died the year before John, and the father is a San Francisco police officer whom I've come to know and admire. Donna and I are sitting at the table with two other couples we haven't met before. I've learned the hard way that these days I don't do well celebrating other peoples' joy. Now, as we're finishing our meal, one of the women is telling Donna about her children. Suddenly she turns to me and asks, "How many children do you have?" Her question, innocent and well-intentioned, flattens me as if I've been run over by a truck. I stumble all over the place and finally tell her I had four but I lost one three years ago. My answer puts a chill on the table conversation, but it's the best answer I can come up with at the moment. I don't know the protocol in these situations. I never knew I would have to know the protocol. I will come to get better at answering that question. I will come to not dread that question. I will come to say, when asked, that I have four children.

On Monday night, as we're clearing away the dinner dishes, Donna says, "The christening was lovely yesterday."

"I'm glad you enjoyed it," I snap back at her.

Her eyes fill with sadness and I realize I've hurt her by snapping. I'm appalled, and I take her in my arms and tell her over and over again that I'm sorry for being such a jerk. In *The Long Goodbye*, Meghan O'Rourke admits that, after the death of her mother, "My grief was not ennobling me. It made me at times vulnerable and self-absorbed, needy and standoffish, knotted up inside, even punitive."

Donna looks at me. "I know you're depressed. You have every reason to be depressed. Maybe you should take a break from all this reading and writing and training about suicide."

I tell her I have to keep going. I hug her again and tell her she's the one who keeps me breathing.

At night prayers we read Psalm 42: " . . . I will say to God my rock, why have you forgotten me?"

* * *

It's Thanksgiving morning, 2011, a little after seven. Donna is still asleep, but I'm awake. This time three years ago, five days before his suicide, John was probably already lost to me. This time three years ago was the last phase of his suffering. This time three years ago I didn't have a clue that he was sinking.

I'm supposed to go to San Quentin for Mass this morning, but I can't move. I have no energy and no desire to go. It seems like a good day to retreat from life and stay under the covers. I also decide I want to change the calendar. Let's just skip everything between Halloween and Groundhog Day.

I hear Donna rustling around in the kitchen with sounds of the Macy's Thanksgiving parade on the television. I finally decide to get up and drive over to the prison. After I've gone through the sally port into the main courtyard I see my friend Ron standing in front of the chapel. He's the inmate I've known here the longest. He's my age, serving a life sentence, still hoping to be released, but aware that he could live out his life inside. He can tell I'm down, and he asks me what's wrong. I tell him what's going on with me, and he leads me into the chapel, over to the far end of the last pew on the right.

We sit down and he says, "I can't be in your shoes, but I've learned that when I get depressed, when things get bad for me, I should try to focus on the positive things in my life, what I can be grateful for." He looks at me and says, "You can be grateful for the time you had with your son. You can be grateful for your other children. You can be grateful for your wife."

I sit there on the wooden pew in this prison chapel, listening to a man who may never get out of here, nicely telling me to get a grip, to get some perspective.

"Mass is starting," Ron says. "Let's sit together."

I follow him up the center aisle and we take two seats on the left in about the eighth row from the altar. When we've settled into our seats, Ron leans over and points to the crucifix behind the altar. "And you can be grateful to Him," he whispers.

During the sermon Father Williams says to the men, "Today is Thanksgiving, and I know that in this place it's easy to focus on what you don't have. But I would ask you to take a moment and focus on what you do have—on what you can be grateful for: your faith, your family, your friends, the programs here that will help you get out of this place." Ron elbows me. I look at him and he's smiling. "See, that's all I was trying to tell you," he whispers.

* * *

On the Sunday after Thanksgiving I go to bed at eleven and fall into a deep sleep. The ringing of my cell phone on the nightstand wakes me up; I turn on the light and see that it's two thirty. I pick up the phone. "Brian, it's Teresa Jeglum," I hear. Teresa is the San Jose PD sergeant in charge of the crisis management unit, and at this time of the night I'm pretty sure she's not calling to see how I'm doing. The knot in my stomach forms even before I'm completely awake.

She tells me that an officer has committed suicide a few hours earlier, and asks me if I can come down and be with the Chief, Assistant Chief, psychologist, and chaplain when they inform all the department officers. Donna wakes up when she hears me talking on the phone. I hang up and tell her about the newest suicide and what Teresa's asking me to do. I say that I don't want to go, but Donna looks at me, senses that I need to go, and says, "Yes, you do." I know she's right.

So I get dressed, jump in my car, crying and praying for the officer and his family. I'm in San Jose a little after three thirty. Teresa is waiting for me at the front door of the San Jose PD headquarters. We go inside, go up a flight of steps, and walk down a long corridor. Teresa tells me that the officer who shot himself used to be in motors with John. He was a midnight patrol sergeant. I don't recognize his name. Teresa then shares with me that he was having marital problems and got into an altercation with his estranged wife on Sunday evening. He strangled her to death, texted some relatives that "things got out of hand," then turned his gun on himself. He left two teenage sons.

As we approach Teresa's office, I'm starting to have trouble breathing. We go into her office and the department senior chaplain, whom I remember from the day I learned about John, greets me. Teresa and the chaplain thank me for coming and introduce me to the department psychologist, who will lead the briefing sessions. All the department's officers are going to be briefed, starting with the day shift when they come in for roll call, and we are to make ourselves available to them. The midnight shift cops will be briefed in a separate meeting when the day shift cops have relieved them. Later there will be a briefing for the investigation units and the swing shift when they come back on duty. I'm going to be part of all these sessions. I ask Teresa dubiously if my presence will be of any value to the officers.

She looks at me with a sad smile. "I'll make sure they know who you are. Your being here will mean a lot to them."

Eventually the chief joins us, shakes my hand, and announces that it's time for the first briefing. I follow Teresa, the chief, and the others down another long hallway till we come to a large conference room on our left. This is the roll call room, where each shift is briefed every day before they go on duty. There are twenty rows of long tables with twelve chairs behind each table. The chief walks to the front of the room and the rest of us take positions standing against the wall to his right. Teresa's on one side of me and the psychologist is on the other. One by one, in groups of three and four, the officers arrive and take their seats. It comes to me that this very room is where John Cahill should have been—where I wanted him to be—when I called the department on the morning of December 4, almost three years ago.

The day shift officers settle into their chairs. There's some talking, but most of the cops are somber and I wonder if some have already heard the news. The chief clears his throat and opens the briefing. He tells the group what's known at this point about the murder/suicide and says that the investigation is being handled by the Gilroy Police Department, where the incident took place, just south of San Jose. Then he introduces those of us standing near the wall. When he comes to me I feel relieved when he mentions my name without referencing John. Teresa and the psychologist speak to the group about the fact that there would be normal and understandable emotional reactions to any tragedy like this; they tell the cops that counseling is immediately available for any officer who wants it and that they shouldn't try to block out their feelings about what happened.

I look across the room at all these cops. They seem so young—not all of them, but many. A lot of them are staring down at the table, shuffling whatever paperwork is in front of them. A few look stunned, but most are showing no reaction. I've been with SFPD officers long enough now to know that when emotional issues arise, their default position is to mask their feelings and maintain a look of impassive neutrality. But as I observe these cops, these protectors, I know there's no way for most of them to completely deny the reality, the horror, of what just happened to one of their own. They must all, to one degree or another, have known the cop who killed his wife and then himself. I imagine they're putting themselves in his place, feeling shock, grief, nearly unbearable empathy, then possibly suppressing those feelings. I can imagine how they feel because I've felt that way myself when I've imagined what John went through, and I wonder if this is how they might have reacted too when they heard about John almost three years ago.

An hour later there's a briefing for the midnight shift as those officers come off duty. Their reactions are the same as what I saw in the earlier briefing. My reactions are also the same. Then there's more time before we meet with the detectives. I walk down the corridor outside Teresa's office to stretch my legs. I spot Steve Guggianna, one of John's close SJPD friends and one of his pallbearers, walking toward me. I had lunch with Steve a year and a half ago, and he told me that one day shortly before John's death they passed each other in the headquarters garage, each of them in a separate patrol car. Steve was going off duty and John was just starting his shift. Steve stopped, waved at John, rolled down his window, and asked John how he was doing. John slowed down and waved back at Steve but motioned that he didn't have time to talk and pulled away. I remember the sadness in Steve's eyes when he told me about that when we were having lunch. Now, as we shake hands in the corridor, Steve tells me he's been called in because he's a member of the department peer support team. He puts his arms around me and says, "I'm glad you're here. Your son is proud of you." I can't speak so I just hold onto him.

At the briefing for the investigation units, most of the thirty to forty officers are wearing shirts and ties. A few are in casual street clothes. They all seem preoccupied; some are carrying thick case files. The presentations by the chief, Teresa, and the psychologist are the same, but the entire session is shorter than the other two. At the end of the briefing most of the investigators immediately take off, and I realize that unlike the cops who work shifts and can let everything go, at least for a short while, these officers probably never get much of a break. They're responsible for multiple ongoing cases. The cases don't go away. These cops might feel the same horror and empathy that the other officers feel, and they might mask it the same way, but uppermost on their minds is getting back to work.

Shortly before noon, after the investigations briefing, I sit in Teresa's office with the psychologist. The psychologist is an attractive middle-aged woman in a navy-blue suit; she has short light brown hair and kind eyes. She hesitates a moment, then tells me that she led the department briefings when John took his life. She puts her arm on my shoulder and says, "That day I talked with most of the officers who knew John. They all said that he was a great cop and a great friend, thoughtful, loved, and respected." I thank her, feeling both gratified and horrified—gratified because she just confirmed my perception of John, horrified because she's brought me back to December 4, 2008, the day after John's death, and I'm slammed all over again with the reality that my son put a bullet in his head and he is gone and I can't reverse it.

Teresa comes back in the office, takes one look at me, and tells me I don't need to stay for the swing shift briefing. I don't argue with her. She walks me out to my car and gives me a hug. I get in my car, exhausted and depressed. I drive the first leg of the trip home wishing that John Cahill were still alive, still a great cop and great friend, still thoughtful, loved, and respected.

Then, all of a sudden, I start to feel relief. I'm puzzled, and then I realize I'm relieved because I'm not the father of the officer who just strangled his wife and then shot himself; relieved that John, no matter how upset he was with Michele, didn't act on his anger. And John *was* angry. They both were. I don't believe John would have been capable of doing what this officer did. But then I'm sure the father of this officer never thought his son could do what he did. And neither one of us thought our sons would commit suicide. This feeling of relief is sudden, intense, and unexpected. Since John died, I haven't felt relief about anything except being retired. I never thought I would feel fortunate in any way related to John's suicide, that there could be anything worse than what happened to him. But everything is relative, and something worse can always happen. Now I see that something worse could have happened to John, and I feel—like a brief rush of warm air—this sudden and fleeting relief.

* * *

The next morning I wake up and see Donna standing over me, looking down at me with a smile. She's dressed for work. I look at the clock. It's eight thirty.

"You took a long time to get to sleep last night, so I turned off the alarm," Donna says. She sits on the side of the bed and strokes my cheek. "I want to tell you how proud I am of you, not just for responding to the SJPD tragedy, but for the way you've responded to God's call to serve in the context of John's death." She kisses me, tells me she loves me, and takes off for work. I lie there, not so sure that she's right, not so sure that I've responded so well to my son's suicide. Most of the time I still feel like I'm stumbling through the days. I'm blessed with Donna, but I have to watch out that I don't drag her down. There are days when I can accept and live with John's death, and there are days when it's so unacceptable, so painful, so depressing, I still feel like I can't breathe, and I don't want to be around. It's not that I want to kill myself. I just don't want to function. That's the real reason why staying under the covers in the morning and staying in the shower at midnight are so attractive.

That afternoon I pull into the parking lot at the San Francisco Police Academy. I know that for today's training session I have to tell the class about the SJPD officer and what he did. It's the last thing I want to do. I sit in my car, wanting to turn around and go home. I realize even more clearly today that this latest cop suicide—in this case a murder *and* a suicide—has brought me all the way back to those first weeks after John took his life. I'm not feeling exactly the same as I did then—I couldn't—because then I was in shock. I'm not in shock now, but I'm remembering that feeling of panic, of not being able to breathe, that sense of horror.

I finally get out of the car and walk into the classroom. Mary Dunnigan takes one look at me and asks me what happened. I fill her in. She looks at me with sad eyes, gives me a hug, and says, "I'm sorry you had to deal with that, but it's a good thing you were down there to support those officers." Then she says, "We can get discouraged or we can work harder. Let's work harder."

In front of the group, Mary does the first part of the training and then hands it over to me. I begin the session by telling the cops sitting in the room the details of this new suicide. I can see some of them reacting with the same horror I'm feeling, especially when I mention the strangling. One African-American woman officer covers her face with her hands. I rush through my prepared comments about John and what can happen when a cop gets depressed and how destructive the job can be to a cop's personal life. Something makes me stop and look up at my audience. "I didn't know this SJPD officer, but I'll bet you anything that two years ago, even if his marriage was going south, this officer, this father of two sons, would never have believed that he could so lose his way." I pause. "This can happen to any of you." I can't say any more, so I stand there silently for a moment. Then I walk back to my seat.

Mary gives the officers a break. None of them says anything to me as they walk out of the classroom. There is nothing to say.

15

Finding Forgiveness

LATER THAT WEEK I have lunch with a man I know slightly through my last job. He's a well-known Catholic businessman who was a donor to Catholic Charities during my time there. His forty-two-year-old son took his life three months ago, and a mutual friend asked if I would be willing to talk to him about how I've dealt with John's death.

We meet for lunch in the dining room of a private golf club where the man is a member. After we've been sitting at the table for a while I notice a group of eight women having lunch at another table. Most of them are donors and volunteers at Catholic Charities, and they know both of us. I soon realize, by the way they're looking at us, that they know why we're together and what we're talking about. A few of them wave at both of us. Two of them get up and come over to say hello. I don't know what this man is feeling at this moment. I feel the genuine love and concern of these women, but at the same time I wish to hell I was not on the receiving end of their sympathy. I can't stand this sympathy—not because it isn't genuine and well-intentioned, but because it sets me apart from everyone else; it puts a spotlight on my loss, on the horror of what has happened.

This man is the fifth parent I've met, or met with, who's lost a child to suicide. As he tells me his story I'm struck by his detachment; it's almost as if he's describing the suicide of someone else's son. Then I realize he's still in shock, because it's only been three months for him. I tell him John's story and that I've learned the research shows that most people who commit suicide—not just cops but almost everyone who does it—believe they're a burden, and those who love them will be better off when they're gone. I tell him that a friend of mine who lost an adult child told me the pain of John's death would be with me every day—there's no choice about that, but there is a choice: to retreat from life or to figure out a way to live life in honor of the person we've lost. I tell him that I finally decided to honor John by trying to write about what happened and by doing suicide prevention training to help other cops, and that both these efforts have brought me some healing and peace. I know it's probably too early for him to hear it, but I try to tell him that some grace can come out of this horrible loss.

I sit there, feeling unsure about whether I'm helping him, looking at his sad eyes, knowing he's overwhelmed, that he's trying to figure out what happened to his son, trying to understand what can never be completely understood. I notice that the women are leaving the restaurant. They wave at us. We wave back. I'm glad they're on their way. I don't want any more sympathy, no matter how well-intentioned.

I look at my lunch partner and realize that he's too burdened, too numb, to be grateful or upset about the support and sympathy of these women. As we leave the restaurant and walk to our cars, I try to tell him that when the shock begins to dissipate the real, unfiltered pain will set in. Even though he's already in a lot of pain, I feel like I should warn him about what will happen when the shock wears off, so he won't be surprised when the pain gets worse. I feel like this is something he needs to know, but somehow I can't get the words out. Then I realize that this father will probably have to learn that the hard way, just like I did. My counselor Janet had tried to warn me, but I hadn't believed the pain could get any worse. It did.

Later that day I take a walk out at Fort Funston, the last place John and I walked together. I stand there looking at the gray ocean, the gray and gloomy sky, knowing that my lunch partner is just beginning his grief journey. For him it's been three months. For me it's been almost three years. And it still hurts like hell.

The father I had lunch with talked about what he wished he had said to his son. Now I stand on the bluff looking out at the ocean, and I start thinking about all the things I wish I had said to John. I wish, when he mentioned having suicidal thoughts, I had looked him in the eye and asked him if he was seriously considering suicide. I wish I had gone down there and grabbed him and made him promise to call me whenever he began to have those thoughts. I wish I hadn't assumed then that he was doing all the right things. I wish I had known more about the medications he was taking. I wish I had called him the week before Thanksgiving. I wish, when he gave his off-duty gun to Bruce, I remembered that he had access to other guns. I wish I had tied him up and played a continuous tape of my voice saying how much he was loved, how much Krissy and Kaitlin needed him to stay alive and be their dad in this life, how much I would help him get through that tunnel of pain and despair and shame, and how much I would help him come out the other end.

I've had these wishes, these thoughts and regrets, many times before. But today, even as I'm wishing them, I realize that some of them, maybe most of them, have never been realistic. And I'm beginning to realize that even if I had done all those things, I might not have been able to stop John. Still, I can't quite let go of that list of things I wish I'd said or done differently. In the next few months I'll read *Paula*, Isabel Allende's haunting memoir about the death of her daughter. She writes about hearing her daughter say to her—"say" in the way John said things to me after he died—"Don't torture yourself thinking of what could have been, things you wish you had done differently, omissions, mistakes . . . Get all of that out of your head!"

I'm still trying to get all of that out of my head.

* * *

A few mornings later I get up and go to San Quentin. Today is the day three years ago when the doorbell rang and the team of San Jose cops told me about my son. But I'm not immobilized. I want to go to the prison. My reasons are selfish. I'm not going to support the guys. I'm going to get support from them, to get grace from them. As I walk into the prison courtyard, four of the men I know well are standing by the front door of the chapel, all wearing freshly ironed, prison-issue blue denim shirts, all waiting to greet me with sad smiles. They know what day this is. We walk into the chapel with two men on either side of me—my protectors—and we sit together. At Mass during The Prayers of the Faithful all the men in the chapel pray for "John Cahill, on the third anniversary of his death."

I look around at all these lifers who have committed serious felony crimes, and I think of my own life. Entering into my first marriage completely unprepared as a husband and father was not a felony, but the consequences have been pretty destructive. And of course, failing to stop John from committing suicide wasn't a felony. But perhaps it should be, I think. In the moment I don't even realize what a crazy thought this is, but later as I'm driving away from the prison I realize it is a little weird. I know that my failure to see where John was at the end—my failure to stop him from ending his life—is not legally a crime, and it's definitely in a different ballpark from the offenses of the men I just left. And yet I've often told the guys in the spirituality group, "We all screw up. Some of our screw-ups are felonies and some are not. But they all have consequences." It's no comfort to me that my failure was not a felony. Maybe it wasn't even a screw-up. But it definitely had consequences.

* * *

On a Tuesday in January 2012, I go to the San Francisco Police Academy for another training session. Before the session starts Mary Dunnigan introduces me to a recently retired SFPD sergeant, Ed Anzore, a veteran of twenty-nine years on the streets of San Francisco. He's a tall, broad-shouldered, gray-haired fifty-something, and he has cop written all over him. Mary has told me that he's written about his depression in the department newsletter and she asked him to come and speak to the class today. I look at this tough-looking man and struggle to envision him talking about his fears, being that vulnerable in front of his peers. Mary has scheduled him to speak right after me.

After I finish Ed gets up and says, "My career as a cop is no better than any other cop's. But I now realize that as a young man and even into my forties, the violence I experienced as a cop left a real impact on me. It caused me to freeze up, to not feel or express emotion, to not be a good husband." Every cop in the room is focused on him, listening to his every word.

He describes some of his experiences and talks honestly about his depression, his suicidal thoughts, his eventual realization that he was dealing with post-traumatic stress, and his decision to finally ask for help. He is strong, credible, courageous, and honest, and I can see that he has a powerful impact on the officers.

When the program is over a number of cops come up to greet their friend and colleague and thank him. After the officers leave Ed and I stand at the back of the room talking. Like me, I learn, Ed is a native San Franciscan who grew up out in the Sunset district, near the beach.

When Mary Dunnigan comes over and asks him if he would like to speak at this session every week, he looks at me as if asking whether I think he should. I nod and say, "You absolutely have to do this. Not only will these guys listen to you, but we can also be a team. I can tell them about the worst thing that can happen when a cop gets depressed, and you can tell them there's a solution."

Ed agrees, and we become partners, trying every Tuesday afternoon after that to help cops understand the hidden risks of their work.

One night at dinner I tell Donna that I really like working with this retired officer who is willing to get up there and tell his story. But whenever I'm with him he reminds me that John is gone. The issue isn't physical resemblance—he doesn't look like John—but when he gets up and tells his story I want to scream. It's not that I don't want him up there, I just want John to be up there telling his story, how he got help for his depression, how he survived.

Donna looks at me with concern. "You need to see Janet." I tell her that I can't keep going back to Janet every time I have a problem. She drops her fork on her plate and says with love—and, I can tell, with some exasperation—"You have more than one problem. You're doing the police training every week and paying a price for it. You've been hurt and depressed by the suicide of that San Jose officer six weeks ago. You just got through the third anniversary of your son's death. You're still beating yourself up for not saving John, even though a part of you knows you couldn't have saved him. You still feel like you've failed as a parent with all your kids from your first marriage. And even though I told you not to, you're still reading all that suicide and grief literature. Get your butt to Janet!"

Two days later I drive to Janet's office. This time the waiting room is empty. I take that as a good sign. I tell her what's going on. Then I reach for the Kleenex. Janet reminds me that each time I do the training I'm re-traumatizing myself. She knows I'm not going to stop the training or the writing, but she makes me promise to stop reading about suicide. She also points out that the recent SJPD murder/suicide has piled more trauma onto me and added to my depression. But even without those factors, she says, the third anniversary is always painful, and only after a few more years will this time of the year become a little easier.

Regarding what I didn't do or say the month before John took his life, and especially my being so passive when he told me he was giving up his off-duty weapon, Janet reminds me that I only knew what I knew, that I was correct back then about suicidal ideation not necessarily leading to suicide, and that on the surface John did look like he was "doing all the right things." She also tells me that I was John's father, not his counselor, and that he never would have let me be his counselor; he knew how much I loved him, and therefore my love and concern for him were in no way passive. In terms of my feeling like a failure as a father, Janet says feeling that way is part of the loss of perspective that arises from being completely drained; being drained emotionally leads to fatigue, and that fatigue leads to depression. She reminds me that I have to continuously ask myself what I need to do to take care of myself, and that's not selfish—it's necessary. She grabs my arm and says, "And stop beating yourself up. You didn't fail, and you did the best you could with John." I'm still not so sure.

I also fill her in on being able to see Kaitlin and on our reconciliation with Michele and having Krissy and Kaitlin back in our lives.

Janet looks at me and says, "You've played a role in some significant healing."

My own thinking is that, along with God's grace, Donna has contributed to most of that healing, and while I'm relieved and grateful for what has happened, I'm pretty sure that in terms of healing, I will need to be on the receiving end of it for some time to come.

Pain and grace are my constant companions, locked in some symbiotic relationship I'll never completely understand. I do know that no matter how much grace I receive there will still be pain, and no matter how much pain I experience there will still be grace.

And no grace or healing can obliterate the reality of suicide. In *The Suicide Index*, Joan Wickersham, referring to her father's suicide, writes, "Knowing that if I could somehow get him back, rewind the tape, look him in the eyes and say, 'Please don't do it,' he might look away from me and do it anyway."

I have to acknowledge that John, no matter how connected he was to me, no matter how much I was his rock, might have looked away and done it anyway, even if I'd had the opportunity to look him in the eyes and ask him to please not do it.

* * *

On a Tuesday night in early 2012, eleven men show up in the San Quentin chapel for the spirituality group. It's raining, and they take off their prison-issue yellow rain jackets and fold them over the back pew near our circle of chairs. For the past few weeks we've been discussing the power of forgiveness. The guys have been pretty comfortable with the topic, but tonight I remind them that we're going to talk about forgiving ourselves. It's clear from the looks on their faces that they're less comfortable with this aspect of forgiveness. As we talk some of the men quietly admit that they haven't been able to forgive themselves, and as I sit there listening I realize that I'm no different, and that the blind are leading the blind this evening.

Finally Clint, the tall gray-haired lifer who a while back urged me to forgive Michele, speaks up and reminds us of his past. "I committed murder when I was sixteen. I took a person's life. I destroyed a family. For a long time I hated myself. But the more I learned about God, the more I began to pray, I realized that God forgives us no matter what we've done." He pauses and says, "I want to read my favorite line in the Bible. It's from Psalm 103. I know we reflected on this a while back in one of our sessions, but I think it's worth going over again." He reads: "As far as the east is from the west, so far does God remove our sins." He looks up and says to the group, "If God can forgive us, we should be able to forgive ourselves."

Clint is well-respected by the other men. His comments break the ice, and soon most of the men in the group are sharing their thoughts. After the group is over, Clint comes up to me. I've been open with the group about how I feel about my failure to stop John from taking his life, so Clint knows that tonight's topic applies to me as much as it does to the men in blue. He puts his hand on my shoulder and says, "I don't think you did anything in terms of your son that requires God's forgiveness, but you need to forgive yourself. You need to get with the program."

I look up at him. My wife has told me I have to forgive myself. My counselor has told me I have to forgive myself. And now I'm standing in a prison chapel and a convicted murderer is telling me that I have to forgive myself. But if I'm honest I have to recognize that I'm not there yet. I would like to get there, but it still seems a little self-serving, a little too easy, just to say, "I forgive myself."

I take a deep breath and tell him, "I'm working on it."

A year later Clint will be paroled, working for a catering company at the airport and living in a tiny studio apartment that he will cheerfully assure me is "way bigger" than his cell at San Quentin.

16

John Is Here with Us

MARCH 30, 2012, IS John's forty-sixth birthday. The Morning Prayer reading is from Psalm 31: " . . . my rock, my refuge . . . " On the night of the thirty-first I dream of John. He is ten years old. He has just been to the barber, and he's upset at the way his hair looks. He's not crying, but he's very angry and frustrated. I hug him and tell him his hair is wet and slicked down, but when it dries it will look fine. He looks up at me and calms down. I see his ten-year-old face so clearly. I wake up and look at his picture on my nightstand, a picture taken a few months before he died. When I was dreaming I saw his ten-year-old face and now, in the picture, I'm seeing his forty-two-year-old face. As I look at it I feel his spirit, right here, up close. I can't see it, but I can feel it. I can feel him, in some real way I can't describe.

On May 10, 2012, Donna reads morning prayers and a passage from First Corinthians: "No trial has come to you but what is human. God is faithful and will not let you be tried beyond your strength, but with the trial, He will also provide you a way out, so that you may be able to bear it." I think that if I had read this in the first couple of years after John died I would have told St. Paul to shove it. But something is happening. I'm beginning to bear it.

* * *

A few days later we drive down to Kaitlin's first dance recital at her high school. Michele is waiting for us out in front of the school. We walk into the auditorium together half an hour before curtain time. Most of the seats are already filled, and there's a buzz of conversation and laughter from the eager parents, siblings, and classmates of those performing tonight. The dancers are all backstage, so we don't get to see Kaitlin before the show starts, but a number of her classmates come rushing up to Michele, hug her, and tell her they'll be cheering for Kaitlin. We find three seats in the back row and sit down with Donna between Michele and me. Someone lowers the lights and suddenly I find myself so aware of John's absence, so depressed that he's not here to see his daughter dance, so distraught that he's not sitting next to me, that before I know it I'm back in the horror and despair of the first six months after he shot himself.

The lights go completely out and I sit there fighting back tears. Then the curtain goes up and there's Kaitlin on the stage, among some other girls, poised to begin; she's in the first number, a dance from *The Lion King*. The music starts, and the girls begin to dance. Donna grabs my arm, and I realize she's crying, too. She whispers, "Listen to the words." The song is *The Circle of Life*:

> It is the circle of life and it moves us all
> Through despair and hope, through faith and love
> Until we find our place on the path unwinding
> In the Circle of Life.

We look at each other. It's no coincidence that this song is playing this moment. Donna knows why I'm crying and she's still holding onto my arm. "See, John *is* here!" she whispers in my ear. I look at Kaitlin dancing on stage and it comes to me in that moment that Donna's right: John is not absent. He's sitting next to me; he's seeing his daughter dance. He is with us, watching over us. Always.

Kaitlin's group does a few more numbers, and they're wonderful, but I don't pay much attention to the music or lyrics or even the dancing. All I know is that John's spirit is still here, and I'm reminded once again of the unavoidable connection between pain and grace.

I also know by now that I will not always receive that grace. Sometimes it feels like the Grace Giver is not delivering on certain days. And I know it's possible that grace comes by and I miss it in my pain and depression. Or, more likely, I miss it during those times when I slip back into thinking I'm in control. From now on, I decide, I'll try to keep my eyes open, or my heart, my soul—whatever works.

* * *

In late September Donna is busy at work, and I decide to drive up to the mountains by myself. I stop at Rainbow Pool on the South Fork of the Tuolumne River. In my mind's eye I see my sons jumping off the thirty-foot-high rock next to the waterfall when they were kids. I see LeAnn with her arms around my neck as we swim under the waterfall. I drive by our old campground on the Middle Fork of the Tuolumne River. I see Ed with a proud smile on his face, holding his fishing rod and a ten-inch rainbow trout, larger than anything his brother had caught that day. I keep driving, stop at Camp Mather, park the car, and get out and walk down to Birch Lake. There, in my mind's eye, I see John stalking frogs at the edge of the lake. I stay at Evergreen Lodge that night, and the next day I climb up to the spot overlooking the Tuolumne Gorge, where we distributed John's ashes. I don't say anything to John, silently or aloud, because I've already said it all. I just want to be with him, in the only way that I can.

In *A Grief Observed* C.S. Lewis writes about his deceased wife, "She seems to meet me everywhere." Mary Allen writes about her lost fiancé, "I feel his presence in many small, ineffable ways." Now I'm looking down the Tuolumne River where John and I rafted, looking upriver where we fished, and further upriver toward Hetch Hetchy where we backpacked, and I meet John everywhere. I feel his presence. I drive back to Evergreen, hit the bar, and raise a Jameson to John Francis Cahill.

That night in my cabin I read night prayers, and the intercessions include, " . . . for all parents who suffer over their children's life choices, for all parents who mourn the death of a child."

The next morning I wake up around seven. Some mornings I have a few seconds before John's suicide assaults me, but today there's no gap between my sleep and the reality of his death. I shower, dress, and walk from my cabin to the dining room. I have no appetite, so I just order a cup of coffee and take it out on the long front porch of the lodge. I sit in an oversized wooden Adirondack chair looking out at the pine trees.

This morning, unlike yesterday, and unlike that night when Kaitlin danced, I don't feel John's presence in any way. I don't meet him anywhere. It's been almost four years, and it still hurts. It's going to continue to hurt. There's no panic now, and there's less horror, but there's still a gaping hole.

My eye falls on a six-foot pine tree near the edge of the porch, and I think of the pine that was planted on the site where John shot himself. I wonder if that tree is thriving in that ground. I haven't been back to that place in some time. I'm not sure I want to go back.

I finish my coffee, check out, and begin the drive home. This is definitely a day when I'm not feeling John's presence. But even in my gloom, I know that I've felt his presence many times, especially at Kaitlin's dance recital, and I'm confident that I will again. And I know, too, that I'll have more days like this morning—not meeting him anywhere, not feeling his presence, only feeling his absence, revisiting what he did—facing the gaping hole, confronting the pain.

In *Healing Through the Dark Emotions*, Miriam Greenspan makes a powerful and compelling appeal for us to aggressively confront our suffering as the most effective and healthy way to grieve and to heal. She writes from the painful perspective of her own child's death about the abruptness with which life can change. In her view no one gets away without suffering. Dark emotions don't go away, but if we stay fully aware of them they can move us through our suffering. Greenspan believes that we have to make meaning out of our suffering or we will be lost. For Greenspan, "Faith is choosing life despite it all, in the teeth of it all."

She's right, but it's easier to choose life on some days than on others, and as I leave the mountains and begin to cross the San Joaquin Valley, heading back home to San Francisco, I feel what I've been feeling ever since I woke up this morning: This is not one of the easy days.

* * *

I wake up on Monday, December 3, 2012, knowing that four years ago today was the last day of my son's life. I'm also depressed because I learned yesterday that another San Francisco police officer just committed suicide. He had been scheduled to attend my class at the police academy in two weeks. I sit on the side of my bed feeling heavy and remembering how I couldn't breathe when I first learned John was gone.

Later, when we're sitting at the kitchen table, Donna reads morning prayers. The first reading is from Psalm 27: " . . . On a rock he sets me free . . . " The second reading is from Isaiah: " . . . Upon those who dwelt in the land of gloom, a light has shone. You have brought them abundant joy and great rejoicing." Then Donna declares that we will no longer refer to this day as the anniversary of John's death. I look at her, puzzled. She smiles and says, "From now on this day will be 'His Soul Never Touched the Ground Day.'" A minute later I feel the heaviness lift off my shoulders, and I realize I'm breathing easier.

And reflecting on Psalm 27 and on Isaiah, I also realize—perhaps fully for the first time—the value and power of the readings we have done as part of our morning and evening prayers these last four years. It's not just that I appreciate that Donna has been having us do this shortened version of the Liturgy of the Hours, a way that the medieval monks sanctified each part of the day; it's that I have finally internalized how God communicates to us through these scripture readings and prayers, finally understanding and accepting that these prayers have been for me a special healing tool of connection with God and John.

I go to Mass and to the gym, come home and shower, then drive down to the Mountain View Police Department, forty miles south of San Francisco, to give the same suicide prevention talk I do every week for SFPD. Ellen Kirschman, who has written extensively on the emotional pitfalls for police officers and their loved ones, and trains a lot of Bay-area police departments, has asked me to join her in this session. When I agreed to give this talk I knew it would be scheduled for the first Monday in December, but at the time I didn't realize that it was going to be on John's death anniversary. When that dawned on me two weeks ago, I was thrown. I'd spent each of the last three anniversary dates with Donna, protecting myself and taking shelter from the world. But now, as I drive to Mountain View, I'm clear about the fact that today I want to help other cops and honor my son. Donna offered to go with me, but for some reason I know I'll be able to do it alone.

When I arrive at the police department I realize that my presentation today will be different from my normal one, because in addition to speaking to police officers, I'll also be speaking to spouses and family members. I look out at the audience and I can tell who the cops are. They're in their thirties and early forties, both the men and women alert and physically fit. Many of the men have closely-cropped hair and mustaches—just like John did.

I tell John's story. I don't have the PowerPoint presentation with photos of him that are onscreen when I do this at SFPD. Today, I pass out a file folder of eight-by-eleven pictures of John as an infant, teenager, cop, father, and son. But I make sure not to look at the photos. I tell my audience that if this can happen to my son, it can happen to any officer anywhere. In the last few years it has happened in San Jose three times and in San Francisco four times. According to the Badge of Life, each year across this country, 150 cops commit suicide.

Most of the officers and some family members come up and thank me afterward. One young officer takes me aside and tells me he has a brother who's also a cop and going through a painful divorce and financial disruption. I see the worry in his eyes, but he thanks me and tells me that now he knows what to say to his brother. He will tell him what can happen to cops when they get depressed, especially when they've lost a relationship, tell him that asking for help is not a sign of weakness but a sign of strength and courage, and tell him that he'll help him find the right counselor so he can get the help he needs and get through this tough time in his life.

I drive back to San Francisco and meet Donna at the Cliff House, a restaurant overlooking the Pacific Ocean, for dinner. On this day she wants us to be near the soothing sound of ocean waves. Donna raises her glass, and we toast John Francis Cahill. Then she tells me that both our grand-daughters have posted messages about their dad on their Facebook pages. We had dinner with them last night to help all of us get through the anniversary. Donna gently reminded them how much their dad loved them and that he's with them and still loves them. Last night, more than any time since John died, I felt that our collective need to be together—Donna and I and the girls—is not just driven by our love for each other; it's driven by our sense that in being connected to each other we're connected to John. Krissy wrote on her Facebook page, "I can't believe it's been four years. I love you and miss you." Kaitlin wrote, "I love my dad, John Francis Cahill."

At the Cliff House Donna and I have our coffee after dinner, listening to waves breaking below us. I look at my wife—this beautiful, evolved soul; this intuitive, sensitive partner; this wise, loving grandmother—and I'm reminded again that she's the reason I'm still breathing. "His Soul Never Touched the Ground Day." Another day of pain and grace.

* * *

It's December 22, 2012, and we're in the kitchen preparing dinner. Donna's excited that Krissy and Kaitlin are coming up to celebrate an early Christmas with us. The Christmas holidays are not my favorite time, but if anything can cheer me up, it's time with my granddaughters. The doorbell rings, and Donna beats me to the front door. She opens the door and Kaitlin is standing on the step with a huge four-foot-tall, four-foot-wide, and six-inch-deep white box. Behind her are Krissy and her boyfriend, Clinton. Krissy is carrying a shopping bag that's almost as large as Kaitlin's gift. They all come in, put down the presents, and give us each a hug. They're eager for us to open the gifts. First, I gently pull a handmade wreath sprayed with a white frost out of Kaitlin's box. The wreath is decorated with small colorful ornaments and interspersed through it are photos of the girls and John. I start to cry, so Kaitlin hands the wreath to Donna and then hugs me. "My mom helped me make it," she whispers in my ear.

Krissy kneels down, takes six large wrapped packages out of the shopping bag, and hands them to Grandma Donna. Donna opens them one by one. Each package contains one twelve-inch-high, five-inch-wide, white-painted plaster letter covered with nickel washers and rhinestones. Krissy sets each letter on the coffee table as Donna opens them. Together they spell out C A H I L L. "I made them myself," Krissy says. Her eyes shine as she looks at the letters, and I think of how years ago, when she was in her early teens, she decided to legally change her last name to Cahill. We hug her and thank her. Donna, with tears in her eyes, says to the girls, "There's nothing that you could have given us that would mean more, and there are no other homemade presents that could express pure love more than these do." Donna lines up the letters on the fireplace mantel, and we take our own wreath down and hang Kaitlin's on the front door.

Later, after we've given the girls their presents and finished dinner, Donna tells them that in her father's Slovak Christmas tradition every member of the family expresses a wish for each other family member while breaking them off a piece of bread to eat. When it's Kaitlin's turn to give me a wish, she lowers her eyes and says, "I wish a long life for Grandpa so he can be around for me after I get out of college." Then Krissy looks at me and says, "I wish that Grandpa will be able to write a great book about Dad."

17

John is in His New Life

IN MARCH 2013 I dream that I'm at some kind of conference and I see John. He's with some friends and says he doesn't have time for me. They go into a large dining room, but there's no room for me. I'm hurt, but I don't want to tell John that I'm hurt. Then I decide to go into the dining room anyway, not knowing what I'm going to say, just wanting to have time with him. I enter the room but everyone is gone. I wake up, thinking yet again of that week in November 2008 when I didn't call John.

* * *

Now it's Easter Sunday evening, 2013. I'm sitting at our dining room table closest to the front window. Donna is at the other end, near the kitchen. She's already served the honey-baked ham, scalloped potatoes and string beans. I've poured one of the central coast reds that John loved. My cousin Joan is to my right and our youngest, Danielle, is to her right, next to Donna. Kaitlin is to my immediate left. Krissy is next to her, and then Michele. Ed and Mark are in Tucson with Mark's parents. And I'm painfully aware of LeAnn's absence; she's been out of our lives for a year and a half.

Michele's current husband, a Scotts Valley cop named Dave, is working tonight. I've come to observe that Dave is a good man and a good stepfather to Kaitlin, although there was a time, before I knew him, when I wanted to kick the shit out of him for not being John, for taking John's place. And there may have been a time when he wanted to kick the shit out of me for the way I treated him.

I look at Michele and marvel once again that she and I have forgiven each other. I look at Krissy, my first-ever granddaughter, now a poised young woman starting her career. Then I look at Kaitlin, fifteen, becoming a woman way faster than a grandfather should be expected to handle. I look at her long light-brown hair, blue eyes with a hint of hazel, skin a combination of alabaster and gold. And I think, "John, your daughters are beautiful."

Thanks to a good therapist, Donna, Michele, and God's grace, Kaitlin's talking about her dad these days, about her pain and loss, not burying it, not letting it fester. A few weeks earlier she was with us for a couple of days. She was in my study and saw the folded American flag on my bookshelf, the one I was given at the funeral. "Is that my dad's flag?" she asked me.

I told her it was.

"Will that come to me one day?" she asked.

And I said, "Absolutely."

She looked at me and said, "But I guess you want to hold onto it for a while."

I nodded, but I couldn't get any words out.

Now, on this Easter Sunday evening, I look at my granddaughters and I look at their mom, and I'm amazed at the power of forgiveness. I look around the table. We are a family, what's left of us—imperfect, flawed, still with steep hills to climb, but surviving.

After dinner, Kaitlin and I are sitting on the sofa in the living room, planning her trip to New York. Ed and Mark have invited her to visit them there for a week when school gets out, and she's excited. Kaitlin's a dancer, and she doesn't know that Ed is going to get some Broadway tickets for Cindy Lauper's *Kinky Shoes* and also seats for the Alvin Ailey Dancers. Ed also is planning a tour of the Fordham campus where he's a professor, dinner in the West Village, and a tour of the 9/11 Memorial for Kaitlin's visit.

After we decide on the dates of the trip, airline reservations, and other logistics, Kaitlin puts her head on my shoulder. She's quiet, and after a moment I realize she's crying. I know, without her having to tell me, that she's thinking about her dad.

"Do you want to talk about it?" I ask her.

She scrunches in closer and says in almost a whisper, "He won't be there to meet my first boyfriend. He won't see me in my first prom dress. He won't be able to walk me up the aisle. He won't ever be a grandfather."

I can't breathe, and my tears come. Donna notices us from the dining room, and part of me wants her to come and rescue me. Grandma Donna and Kaitlin are joined at the hip. They have these kind of close, intimate conversations; I'm the ice cream guy, the zoo guy, and the movie guy. I can see *Cars II* three times. But Donna and I exchange looks, and I know from my wife's glance that I have to stay with this, that Kaitlin is sharing herself with me.

I turn my head and look at her. If I feel horror at my son's suicide, what must she and Krissy feel about what their dad did? I stroke her cheek and wipe away her tears with my index finger. I tell her that I'm glad she's facing this and talking about it; that it's healthy and good for her to talk about her dad; that even though it's incredibly painful, it's better to deal with it than to bury it.

She tells me that she has a friend she talks to, and she also talks with her mom. She looks up at me. "And I know I can talk to you guys."

I squeeze her and whisper, "Yes you can. Anytime."

Then I tell her about the training I'm doing with police officers and the book I'm trying to write about her dad and what happened; that this is the way I want to honor my son. I tell her that she has no choice about this pain and loss in her life, but she does have a choice about whether to let her dad's death limit her or live her life as fully as she can, to not just survive but to thrive, to make her dad a witness of hope and life rather than despair and death. I tell her that's what I want for her and that's what her dad wants for her. As I say all this, I know it's not enough. I know there's more work to do. But I'm wiped out now, so I just hold her.

That night, lying in bed, I ask myself if I'm finally feeling any anger toward John. Twice since John has died, I've asked myself if I was angry, and my response was that I thought I understood what had happened to John and therefore I wasn't angry. But after tonight I'm not so sure.

A few days later I drive down and talk to Janet about this. As I tell her what Kaitlin said, she looks at me and says, "What are you thinking and feeling right now?" Before I can think I start to cry and blurt out, "John, what the fuck! How could you do this?"

Janet waits until I stop sobbing and begin to calm down. Then she says, "Anger doesn't change love or reduce love. Anger in this case actually helps. It helps you to acknowledge it and move on, and it helps John spiritually to own it and clear it." Then she smiles at me and says, "You're a real social worker. You're not angry with John for your own pain. You're angry at him for Kaitlin's pain."

As I get back in the car, I realize that just because I've finally discovered my anger, it doesn't mean I have to hold onto it. And Janet is right. It doesn't make me love John any less.

* * *

It's May 2013, and I'm entering Fromm Hall on the campus of the University of San Francisco to witness my friend Lorenzo being honored. Of all the men I've come to know through my time at San Quentin, I feel closest to

Lorenzo. He's insightful and remorseful about what he did, but he's never surrendered to paralyzing guilt the way some inmates I talked to seemed to do. I'm still struggling with my own guilt, and I've come to regard him as a kind of a role model.

Now I see him standing in the aisle halfway down the hall, talking to some friends. He's been out of prison since 2010, and I've had lunch with him three or four times since then. He has the same short brown hair and neatly trimmed beard and mustache he had in prison. But today, of course, he isn't wearing blue prison dungarees. Instead he's in a well-tailored gray business suit, white shirt, and gray-and-red tie. He spots me and comes over. He gives me a bear hug and says, "I'm here because of you."

Twenty-seven years ago Lorenzo was convicted of second-degree murder. Three years ago he was released from San Quentin Prison. One week ago he received his college diploma. Today, as part of a ceremony honoring outstanding students and faculty members, Lorenzo is receiving the University of San Francisco Oscar Romero Award for Outstanding Community Service. For the last two and a half years, not only has Lorenzo been a full-time business major, he's also been an active and committed advocate for restorative justice and for re-entry services for those being paroled from state prison.

I've known Lorenzo since 2005, when I first started volunteering at San Quentin. I know his character, strength, integrity, and spiritual depth. After his repeated parole denials—denials based on no valid reason—I raised some money and found a dedicated attorney who fought successfully for his release. Lorenzo's mother has always been grateful for what I did for her son, and each year around the time of John's death she sends me a note.

Now I'm sitting to the left of Lorenzo and his mom is on his right, on the aisle, near the front on the left side of the hall. When Lorenzo is called up to receive his award, his mom motions to me to move over and sit next to her. "This must feel pretty great," I whisper.

She looks at me with a wide smile, tears sliding down her cheeks, and whispers back, "This is beyond belief." Then she focuses all her attention on her son as he's being introduced on the stage.

I look over at her and think it's doubtful that she ever thought she'd see Lorenzo a free man, let alone a college graduate receiving a high honor. And then I have another thought. She didn't have Lorenzo for twenty-four years, and now she has him. I had John for forty-two years, and now I don't have him.

I look around the auditorium. The place is full of enthusiastic, excited students who are being acknowledged for their accomplishments. I see parents with broad proud smiles. I look back at Lorenzo's mom and realize that her emotions today are unique among all these beaming parents. And I remember John's college graduation, the pride I felt, my sense of comfort because he knew his life's direction. He knew he wanted to be a cop. It never occurred to me on his graduation day that, on another day, far in the future, he would lose his sense of direction.

I think about all of this, and then I look up at Lorenzo, standing on the stage with the other awardees. He has a sense of direction. He has a life to live. This is his day. Lorenzo lost his way, his sense of direction, early in his life. I don't think he'll lose his way again. But now I know that anyone can lose his way.

My firstborn, my rock, lost his way, and unlike Lorenzo he has no second chance to find it again. But then I think—this time without reservations or doubt—that John is in his new life.

I look up at Lorenzo again. After all his pain and suffering and the pain and suffering he caused others, he's found redemption in this life. And with Lorenzo's mother squeezing my hand, I realize that, in different ways, both our sons have found new life.

18

If I Knew Then What I Know Now

THE FOLLOWING TUESDAY I'M back in front of my cops. After I'm done, an officer in his mid-forties comes up to me and asks if we can go outside and talk. Standing in the parking lot behind the classroom building, he tells me his story, a story similar to John's. There's a divorce, serious financial problems, and worry about the impact of the divorce on his children. And then the officer tells me that two years ago he tried to kill himself. He failed in his effort and finally realized he didn't want to die. He looks at me and says, "I'm still struggling, seeing a counselor, on antidepressants, but alive." He points in the direction of the classroom. "A lot of guys in there are in denial, but you're forcing them to look at this issue." He hugs me and starts back into the building. Before he goes through the door he turns around and says, "Thank you and keep it up."

I'm back in my car, thinking about this officer's failed suicide attempt and thinking about John. Why didn't John's attempt fail? Why didn't John's weapon jam that night? Why couldn't John be seeing a counselor, on antidepressants, but alive? But then I think: Glocks don't jam. They get the job done. And John was always organized, competent, and thorough in everything he did, even in the very last thing he did.

And for the first time in four and a half years, I'm finally able to admit to myself that if John had to die, I wish it hadn't been suicide. And then I remember how, when four Oakland police officers were killed in the line of duty a month after John's funeral, I had a twitch of this thought then too, a hint of a wish that John had died in the line of duty. Until now I have never let that thought come close to the surface; I'd always said to myself that the major issue was his loss, the fact that he was dead, that he was gone. How it happened was secondary.

Now I slump in my car, wanting my son not to be a suicide victim. It's not because of the stigma or shame. It's not because I can't understand why it happened. It's not even the horror of him putting a bullet through his head. It's because he was so lost, in so much pain, so distorted in his thinking, that he couldn't see what this could do to Krissy and Kaitlin. And it's because I couldn't stop him. I couldn't protect him. I couldn't be his father.

Of course, I *am* still his father. Donna's been telling me that over and over, and even without her telling me that, part of me knows it. Part of me knows it's a biological, historical fact. Part of me knows that I was a good father to John. Part of me knows that John felt my love and support all his life, and even though it couldn't protect him and sustain him when he entered the last stage of his life, when he descended into that zone of despair and inapproachability, he still knew I was his father. But inescapably now, and maybe for a long time to come—possibly for the rest of my life—I'll be haunted by the fact that fathers are supposed to protect their children.

But can we really protect our children? For that matter, can we really protect cops from killing themselves? Probably not, but there are lots of things we can do to keep some cops from killing themselves, to reduce the number of cops who kill themselves. I've learned this by now.

I'm still in my car, in the parking lot of the police academy. I'm exhausted, depressed, wanting again to retreat from life. I'm supposed to be at the San Quentin spirituality group in a couple of hours, but it's the last thing I want to do. I want to go home and get under the covers; if that doesn't work, I want to get in the shower and stand there till the hot water runs out; and if that doesn't work, I want to get out the Jameson.

Then I remember that every time I go to San Quentin I feel better. So I start my car and head toward the Golden Gate Bridge. I love the guys in the spirituality group, but if I'm honest, I'm not going tonight out of love. I'm going so I can feel better.

I enter the San Quentin chapel; a circle of chairs for the group is set up on the right behind the last pew. Most of the guys are here as well as my fellow volunteers. My friend Rodrigo spots me, gets up, and comes over. Rodrigo is a lifer. As a teenager he was deep into substance abuse and was later convicted of murdering his girlfriend. He's in his late fifties, a long-time participant in AA, a graduate of the Alternatives to Violence program here at San Quentin, and one of the most mature guys in the spirituality group. When he was a child he was closer to his grandfather than he was to his parents, but when Rodrigo was eleven, his grandfather committed suicide. Rodrigo has always been extra-sensitive about my feelings around the loss of John.

"Could we do something different during the last fifteen minutes to-night?" he asks.

"Of course," I answer. "It's your group. What do you have in mind?"

"Gene wants to come in and sing a song he's just written." Gene is the guitarist in the chapel inmate choir and a talented musician.

"What's he going to sing?" I ask.

Rodrigo looks down, hesitates, then he says softly, "Gene has a friend whose twenty-four-year-old brother jumped off the Golden Gate Bridge last summer. Gene's friend told him the story, and Gene wrote a song about it."

I stand there, stunned. All I can think of is that I came over here to feel better, to get away from suicide, to escape. But I look at Rodrigo and say, "If that's what you guys want to do, that's what we'll do."

After we finish our spirituality group discussion, Gene comes in with his guitar, sits down in our circle, and tells us that the young man who killed himself was named Jason—and that Jason's mother has been hearing mes-sages from him. They're not verbal messages, but she believes they're her son's way of telling her that he's safe and at peace, and that he's looking out for her. I realize that most of the guys are stealing glances at me, and before I know it tears are slowly starting to spill over my eyelids and I'm trying to breathe.

In a clear, smooth, baritone voice, Gene begins the first verse of his song: "Dear mother of mine, it hurts to see you cry. Feel me as I wrap my arms around you now. I'm reaching out to the other side. I apologize I left in a hurry." Then Gene moves into the chorus: "I'm watching you, loving you, and guiding you. I'm already home, and you are not alone." The other verses include Jason thanking his mother for her love, letting her know that his spirit is free in God's mercy, and reminding her that "we are all connected." Then Gene concludes with the chorus, which I realize I need to hear again: "I'm watching you, loving you, and guiding you. I'm already home, and you are not alone."

My head is down and I'm crying, but it's dawning on me that I've been given a huge gift. And I know the guys are expecting me to say something. I look at Rodrigo, whom I know thought this up. "Thank you," I say. I look at Gene, the messenger, and say, "Thank you." I look at the rest of these men and tell them what happened today at the police academy. I tell them about finally being able to admit that I didn't want John to have died from suicide. I tell them that I've heard John's voice, so I can believe that Jason's mom has heard her son's voice. And I thank them.

As I walk out of San Quentin I realize that on this day, when I was the lowest I've been in a long time, I've received a powerful, timely message about John's spirit and God's love, and the message, not surprisingly, has come from these men in this place.

The next day I wake up, comforted by the gift from San Quentin, but I still have to process my realization about not wanting John's death to be suicide. It's still rolling around in my head; disturbing, irritating, like an empty bottle rolling around on the floor of my car, something that needs to be secured, put away.

I call Janet and tell her what's going on and that I'm bothered that I was so slow to realize I felt this way.

"Brian," she answers, "you're fine. Suicide grief is long and complex. There's no set routine or schedule for how we deal with this. And there's nothing wrong with you wanting John's death not to be suicide. Trust your feelings and your process."

Before we hang up she says, "John is thinking that you're making something positive out of this, and I know that you're saving lives."

* * *

In late September I'm sitting in the studio of KQED, San Francisco's National Public Radio station. Four Bay-area cops have committed suicide in the last two months. Michael Krasny, host of the Forum Show, is interviewing me. Joining us by phone is Sergeant Mary Dunnigan, head of the SFPD Behavioral Science Unit, and John Violanti, a former police officer and now the leading national researcher in law enforcement suicide. It's an hour-long show, and my job is to tell John's story and summarize my weekly SFPD presentation as well as a recent article I wrote for *CNN Online*. I get through the hour without falling apart, but as I sit there, right after the show has ended and before we get up and say good-bye, I feel relieved that I was able to do this show in a radio studio. There were no cameras. No one could see the tears.

* * *

It's December 3, 2013, the fifth anniversary of John's death. As part of morning prayers we read Psalm 27: "On a rock He sets me safe . . . " Before Donna leaves for work she looks at me and says, "You're okay, aren't you?" I realize I am okay, at least for the moment. I do my SFPD training in the afternoon and spend the evening with the guys in the San Quentin Tuesday night spirituality group. They know what day it is, and they say a prayer in memory of John before I leave. I'm still okay, I realize as I'm driving home.

There have even been a few hours here and there throughout the day when I didn't think about John, a first on the anniversary day of his death.

The next morning I wake up feeling relieved that I got through yesterday in one piece. I'm making progress, I think. I'm in a better place. Later I'm sitting at my desk going over the outline I use for my police suicide prevention presentation to see if there's anything that needs to be updated. All of a sudden I realize there *is* something missing from my presentation. I look at the outline that I've been using for over two years, and I realize I've never told the officers that John told me he had suicidal thoughts and that he had given his off-duty weapon to his close friend Bruce just to be safe.

I've never shared this with the officers. It hits me like a hammer that I've been uncomfortable sharing this detail with the cops I speak to, that some part of me still feels guilty and ashamed that I reacted so weakly and naively to what John told me about having suicidal thoughts and—I realize now—I'm afraid of being judged for that. Before I know it I'm buried in panic and guilt, back in that time five years ago, remembering the times John and I talked after he told me about the suicidal thoughts, remembering that I never asked him if he was still having those thoughts, remembering my stupid optimism that John was strong enough and secure enough to come through this, remembering the moment when they told me he was gone. I sit there at my desk. I know I'm breathing, but I have that same feeling of not being able to breathe that I had five years ago. I try to go about the rest of my day, but the feeling never goes away.

That night I fill Donna in on this realization. We're sitting side by side on stools at the kitchen counter. Donna looks at me and I can see her going into high gear. She takes a breath and reminds me that I specifically asked John if he was okay each time I saw him after he said he was having suicidal thoughts. She also points out that I never stopped trying to help John solve his problems; that my perception of him never allowed me to think he could possibly end his own life; that maybe there was an unconscious fear in me about suicide, but it was buried too deep to be of any use. She stands up, steps across the small space that separates her from me, leans over, and hugs me. "You did what you could with what you knew," she says. Then she urges me to talk with Janet. She also tells me that I do have to add this to the training presentation. "This is really important for those officers to understand. They need to know how easy it is to assume everything's going to be okay."

A day later I'm in Janet's office making liberal use of the Kleenex once again. After I tell her about my meltdown she reminds me that I *had* told John that day—the day he told me about his suicidal thoughts—that I wanted to call him every few hours, but he told me to stick to our regular weekly talk. "Brian, look at me," she says. "I really want you to hear this. First of all, your knowledge of suicide was limited then. Second, you assumed John was engaged with you and you and he were working together to solve the problems. His taking your suggestion and writing his mantras down and taking your check for a new attorney both suggested to you that he was still engaged. Third, you may well have had an unconscious fear about John taking his life, but it was buried so deep it was useless." She pauses to let me take all this in and then continues: "If you had felt he was withdrawn you would have been more alarmed. And today, with what you know, you would react differently—you wouldn't be seduced by reassurances, and your fear wouldn't stay buried."

For the first time in two days I begin to calm down a bit. Janet takes my hands in hers and says, "You need to understand that your meltdown occurred because you were judging your behavior of five years ago by the knowledge you have today, not by what you knew then."

As soon as she says this I realize that's what Donna was trying to tell me last night, too, but I couldn't hear it. I say that to Janet and she smiles and says, "Donna is a wise soul, and she's also right that you should put this in your training presentation." As I'm heading out the door, Janet says, "Brian, I want to tell you one last thing, and I've told you this before. Even if you had asked him, he might not have told you."

I go and get in my car. I drive home feeling no less sad but calmer than I have in the last forty-eight hours.

On the following Tuesday I'm at the police academy standing in front of twenty-five officers. For the last two days I've been practicing what I've added to my talk. I feel nervous and uncomfortable, but I know I have to suck it up and put this one additional message out there. I tell them about the day John told me he was having suicidal thoughts and how he'd given up his off-duty weapon. I shakily tell them about my reaction—or, more accurately, my lack of reaction. I tell them about my perception of John as a survivor, and I also tell them that I never gave any thought to the fact that cops have unlimited access to guns. I look out at my audience, expecting, or perhaps fearing, that I'll see judgment and disapproval on some faces, but all I see is an attentive and sympathetic group of cops.

I take a deep breath and continue. "I regret every day of my life that I didn't ask him if he was still having suicidal thoughts, and if I knew then what I know now I would have been all over him with that question. But I've also learned that even if I had asked him, he might not have told me."

I pause for a long moment and make as much eye contact as I can with as many officers as I can look at in the time I have. "I want to say something else. I want to say to all of you—if you have a concern that a fellow officer could be harboring suicidal thoughts, do not hesitate to ask them. Do not assume everything will work out. Talk to that officer, and if it's appropriate call Mary Dunnigan or one of the other officers in the BSU. You could be saving a life. And one final thought: If I were talking to your parents, spouses and partners and siblings I would tell them the same thing—regarding you."

I finish the rest of my presentation and the officers applaud loudly. I'm drained but relieved that I got through this, and, if I'm honest, I'm relieved that there was no judgment or disapproval. After I'm back in the car I realize I've taken one more step toward forgiveness, one more step on this strange path of pain and grace.

19

Just Tell Us About Your Son
and You'll Be Fine

IT'S LATE WEDNESDAY AFTERNOON, December 11, 2013, and I'm driving to
San Jose. Janet Childs has asked me to be the keynote speaker this year at
the annual candlelight vigil put on by the Center for Living with Dying. I
remember four years ago, the year after John's suicide, when Donna and I
attended this ceremony and Alisa was the speaker. I also remember thinking back then that I couldn't possibly get up there in front of three hundred
people and talk about John.

But now I'm comfortable with the idea. When Janet asked me to speak
I said, "Sure." Donna was going to cancel a work obligation to come with me,
but I told her, feeling a little surprised, that I didn't need her to be there. She
looked at me and smiled. "You're in a better place, Brian Francis."

This year's vigil is in a large church hall, and as I walk into the room
I immediately spot two long tables holding rows of the blue candles in tall
clear glass jars that I remember from four years ago. Janet comes over to
me and gives me a hug. "I knew you'd be speaking here one of these years,"
she says. The hall is filling up, and I take a seat on the far right end of the
third row so I can easily get to the podium. I'm seated next to an attractive
gray-haired woman around my age. Her name is Sandra, she tells me, and
she lost her son in an automobile accident when he was eighteen. She's been
coming to this ceremony for twenty-five years. I tell her about John and that
I'm speaking tonight. She says she's looking forward to hearing what I have
to say.

All of a sudden it dawns on me that, unlike the police officers I speak
to every week, the people in this audience have *all* lost a loved one, and my
story about John is only one of hundreds of stories of trauma, horror, pain,
and loss in this room. Now I'm nervous, feeling unprepared, wondering why

I so willingly agreed to speak. Sandra notices my anxiety, pats me on the arm, and says, "Just speak from your heart, tell us about your son and you'll be fine."

Janet opens the evening by welcoming everyone. She explains the purpose of the vigil: to shed the trauma and reduce the pain of losing a loved one without losing the love, without losing our memories and feelings of closeness to our loved ones who aren't around in physical form any more. Then Janet introduces me, and before I know it I'm up at the podium.

I tell John's story and talk briefly about what I've learned about cops, depression, and suicide. I share what Donna said to me: "John's soul never touched the ground." And I talk about hearing John's voice, especially late at night in the shower. For those who have lost a loved one to suicide, I share what the spiritual writer Father Ron Rolheiser said in his syndicated column: "We should not spend much time worrying about the eternal salvation of those who die by suicide. God's love, healing, understanding, and forgiveness reach into those places where we cannot." I tell the audience that John was not a believer, but he lived a good life and I believe he went right to God.

I mention the suicide prevention training I'm doing as a way to help other cops and honor John. And I try to share with these parents, wives, husbands, sisters, brothers, and children my idea—my hard-won experience—that along with all the grief and pain there can be grace, that grace somehow mysteriously arises out of the worst tragedies, the most unbelievable horrors. Finally, I tell them that my granddaughters, in spite of the gaping hole in their lives—the hole where their father used to be—are surviving and thriving.

I sit down, and a group of police officers, firefighters and paramedics get up and light the community candles on behalf of all first responders. As I sit there I think about a conversation I had recently with a retired police officer who's now a clinical psychologist. Joel Fay is the clinical director of the First Responder Support Network, a group of retired cops and other first responders who came together a few years ago to help cops, firefighters and paramedics deal with critical incident stress and recover from post-traumatic stress disorder. They run training programs in critical incident stress management. They also run the West Coast Post-Trauma Retreat, for first responders whose lives have been impacted by their work experience. Joel had asked me if I would consider joining him in a few of his training sessions, making the same presentation there that I give at SFPD. Until now I've been reluctant to take on any more responsibility, any more assignments telling John's story and summarizing of the grim reality of law enforcement suicide, any more revisiting of the pain and horror of John's death.

But as I sit here watching these vibrant, dedicated cops and firefighters and paramedics light their candles, I realize that I do want to get more involved; I do want to help first responders avoid the hidden dangers in their work; and I do want to continue to honor my son. A few months later I will begin to work with Joel Fay and the First Responder Support Network.

When the first responders have finished lighting their candles, all the rest of the audience comes up. One by one each person files past the table with the candles, recites the name of their loved one, lights a candle, and leaves it on the table. When it's my turn Janet hands me a candle and says, "This one's just for you." Attached to the candle is a tiny card with John's name, written in Janet's handwriting, and a green-and-blue glass angel Christmas ornament. I speak into the microphone: "John Francis Cahill." I light the candle and put it among the others.

At the end of the vigil a woman who looks like she's in her fifties comes up to me and asks if she can tell me about her son. There are tears in her eyes. "Brian was a Scotts Valley firefighter who transferred over to the San Jose Fire Department," she says, and for a moment I'm startled that her son's name was the same as my name. "He went through a bad divorce, with custody issues and financial problems, and eventually he took his life." I'm speechless, not only because there's really nothing I can say about something like that but also because her son's story is so much like my son's story. So I reach out and hug her. We hold each other for a long minute. Finally I say, "Maybe my John and your Brian knew each other in Scotts Valley."

She looks at me and I see a bit of mild impatience in her eyes. "That's not why I came up to you," she says. "I wanted to tell you how much comfort you gave me when you said your son is with God."

I put my hands on both her shoulders and tell her, "Your son and my son are in the same place."

Back in the car heading home, I realize once again that pain and grace are inextricably linked. There's the pain of standing up in front of a group of people telling John's story one more time, the pain of everyone else's loss, the pain belonging to that woman I spoke to at the end. But there's the grace of giving comfort to fellow survivors, the grace of healing over time—and, I realize suddenly, the grace of this moment, the peace of this moment, as I drive north on Highway 280, alone with my thoughts in the car.

Epilogue

IT'S THE WEEK BEFORE Christmas, 2013, and I'm home alone. I'm in the kitchen, wanting a cup of coffee. There's no ground coffee, so I get some beans out of the fridge and pour them into the grinder.

I've never been very skilled in the use of machinery, technology, or appliances. I cook for Donna two nights a week, but I try not to use anything that has to be plugged in. At work I was blessed with a loving, supportive, competent executive assistant. She was my work partner and is still my friend. When something would go wrong with my computer I'd yell "Oh shit," and Dorothy knew that was the signal to come to my rescue. When I retired Donna was still working, and whenever I had a problem with my laptop and yelled "Oh shit," no one came. It was like the tree falling in the middle of the forest. Then Donna would come home in the evening and help me out. Earlier, before I retired, when John was still with us and he heard about these mishaps, he would look at Donna, curl his lips, and say, "My dad has people to do things for him." Then he and Donna would have a good laugh.

Now, standing in my kitchen, I turn on the coffee bean grinder. But I've failed to secure the lid on the grinder and before I know it, ground coffee is flying all over the place—in my eyes, my hair, the cuffs of my pants, the drawers, the counter, the sink, the floor. Finally I turn the damn thing off.

I shake my head to try to get the coffee grounds out of my hair. I take the dishrag out of the sink and begin wiping the grounds off the counter. But the rag is wet and I'm just making more of a mess. Usually when this kind of disaster happens I'm ready to explode. But today I don't blow. Instead I smile. John is standing there. His lips are curled. He's laughing.

His body isn't here. But I can feel him. His spirit is here. He's with me. He's still my rock. I know there will be days when I won't feel his spirit, but now—in this moment—he's with me.

Appendix A

An Open Letter to All Cops

October 1, 2015

MY DEAR YOUNG MEN and women,

This book is about how a police officer's depression can and sometimes does lead to suicide. It tells the story of my son's suicide and the aftermath of that horror and trauma. In different parts of the book I share what I've learned about cops and suicide, drawing from the work of major writers, researchers, and therapists in this field. I'm trying to point out that the things that make you good at what you do—the very things that keep you safe and effective on the street—can, in some cases, lead you down the dark path that my son took.

When I was in the midst of grieving for John, it came to me that I wanted to honor him by putting my energy into trying to help all of you. Now, as I finish writing this story, I feel that desire even more strongly. You spend your days helping and protecting us, willing to put your life on the line for us. Today your job is more difficult than ever, and every decision you make is held up for public scrutiny and judgment. I believe that the great majority of people in this country respect and appreciate you, but I'm not sure you have the opportunity to hear and feel that respect and appreciation. I do know that you get to experience the hate and disrespect that some people on our streets show you.

I want to try to lay out for you here the things you need to know about depression and suicide among police officers, the things you need to look out for, and the things you need to do to survive in your career and retire to a full and joyful life.

I'm not an expert in any of this. I'm not a cop or a psychologist or a researcher. I'm just the father of a cop who lost his way. And I didn't see it coming. Learning about cops and suicide was not part of my retirement plan. But after John's suicide, while I assumed that his divorce and its after-math was a major factor, I found myself wondering whether John's nineteen years as a cop contributed to what happened. I wasn't trying to blame law enforcement. I just wanted to find out why I lost my son this way.

Today I believe that while the pain and disruption in John's life in the aftermath of his divorce were dominant, John's suicide was also linked to his job in ways that weren't obvious. And that belief and what I've learned about cops and suicide motivates me to scream from the rooftops to every one of you who wears a badge and a gun: be careful, be aware of the emotional risks in your work, be aware of how your work can affect your personal life and your family, be aware how being a cop can lead to depression—and, in some cases, self-destruction.

Some of what I'm writing here is a repeat of information from different parts of the book. But I wanted to lay out the basic information and a set of "how to survive steps" in one place, in one chapter. If you don't read the rest of this book, read this chapter.

My first message to you is that if this could happen to my secure, con-fident, adventurous son, this can happen to you, to any of your partners or your team members. And it does.

In the Bay area alone, the San Francisco Police Department has lost six officers to suicide since 2010—three of them retired and three of them active duty officers. San Jose PD lost my son and a woman officer to suicide in 2008, and a midnight patrol sergeant took his life in 2011. Oakland PD lost two officers to suicide in 2013 and one in 2015. The San Mateo County Sheriff's Department lost a deputy at the end of 2013, and Morgan Hill PD lost an officer just two months ago. According to the Badge of Life, a national organization of former police officers dedicated to preventing law enforcement suicide, 150 cops across the country take their lives every year. The Badge of Life reports that police suicide happens at a far greater rate than police homicide or duty-related accidental deaths.

The Badge of Life also reports that for every police officer that com-mits suicide, there are a thousand officers dealing with post-traumatic stress disorder and another thousand cops struggling with marital issues, depres-sion or alcoholism. There are approximately 940,000 police officers in the United States. If the Badge of Life reports are accurate—and I believe they are—this means that up to 30 percent of all working cops are struggling with serious personal problems while they're on the job. I don't say this to stigmatize you, but rather to point out that the career you've chosen, as noble as it is, can change you, can harm you and your loved ones, and, in some cases, destroy you.

Much of the recent research on law enforcement suicide has been conducted by John Violanti, Ph.D., a former New York state trooper who currently works with the Badge of Life and is on the faculty of the School of Medical and Biomedical Sciences at the State University of New York at Buffalo. The research tells us that good cops are highly functioning in all aspects of their life. They are trained to bring control out of chaos. They're willing to risk everything in the critical incident because they know that the critical incident will come to closure; it won't go on forever. These characteristics make for good cops, but these same characteristics can be lethal when a cop gets depressed. They think they're not functioning well, they're frustrated because they can't control things, and they begin to despair because they think their pain—their "critical incident"—will never end. John didn't think he was functioning well in his work and in his personal life. He was wrong, but his sense of self-worth had been so damaged by his personal problems—his divorce and everything that went with it—that he could no longer see the situation clearly. He also told me how frustrating it was for him not to be able to control his situation. And a month before he died he told me, "This will never end." At the time I didn't understand what any of that meant. Now I do.

Again: if this can happen to John Cahill, it can happen to any cop. It can happen to any of you. Until the last eighteen months of his life, John was the most secure, healthy, and vibrant human being I knew. He went from being healthy and vibrant to depressed and despairing to completely losing his way. My perception of my son as secure and healthy and strong didn't allow me to see that he could be capable of suicide.

In Appendix B of this book, I summarize the major books covering the subject of depression and suicide within law enforcement, but here in this open letter I want to briefly emphasize the work of four authors.

Ellen Kirschman is the author of *I Love a Cop*. She does a lot of training with California police agencies. This is the book I would recommend for your loved ones who may not completely understand the nature of your work. Kirschman emphasizes that cops are oriented toward control and can have a distorted but culturally correct sense that they're invincible and independent—or believe that they should be. Kirschman writes, "A cop's distress can result from a tangled series of events, often including a devastating relationship loss and a temporarily hopeless outlook." That was John.

Thomas Joiner is a psychology professor at Florida State University. He wrote *Myths about Suicide*. He points out that in most cases suicide is not an act of cowardice or selfishness. People who commit suicide perceive that they're a burden, that they don't belong, and that those who are close to them would be better off if they were gone. They're wrong, but that is their reality. That was John's reality. That was the reality of many of the cops who lost their way. They were wrong, but they weren't cowards.

Kevin Gilmartin, Ph.D., was a street cop in Tucson, Arizona for twenty years. Today he travels around the country talking to cops, trying to tell them how to survive a police career. He's the author of *Emotional Survival for Law Enforcement*. Every cop should read this book. If I were your father, I would make you read this book. If I were your chief, I would buy this book for you. Gilmartin's main message is that the very things that make you a good cop, keep you safe, and make you effective on the street can screw up your personal life and, in some cases, destroy you. He points out that hyper-vigilance on the job produces a healthy amount of cynicism and mistrust, which is necessary for street survival but can be destructive for personal relationships and family life.

For Gilmartin, police suicide is always job-related. Some time ago I had the opportunity to meet him and tell him about John. I said that I was pretty sure that my son did not suffer from post-traumatic stress disorder (PTSD). I'll never forget the sad look on his face when he said to me, "It doesn't matter; he was a cop for nineteen years, and that was a factor in his death." Recently I came across a study of fifty-seven NYPD suicides between 1985-1994. Sixty percent of those suicides were determined to have been caused by relationship losses. This job can kill you in a lot of different ways.

A La Mesa police captain, Dan Willis, recently wrote *Bulletproof Spirit*, an easy-to-read book full of practical steps you can follow to take care of yourself. Willis writes about warning signs that can lead to disaster: isolation; irritability; difficulty sleeping; anger; emotional numbness; lack of communication; cynicism; distrust and loss of work satisfaction; depression; drinking as a way to deal with the job or as a habit. He recommends that you keep your private life separate from your job and that you maintain control over your finances. Willis emphasizes the importance of regular exercise, a healthy diet, and moderate use of alcohol and caffeine. He asserts that to be able to survive the stress and trauma of your work, you have to increase your self-awareness "so that you will know when your spirit is suffering from the toxic effects of the job."

I have just a few more thoughts for you. If the issue I'm talking about here—the risk of suicide among cops—is taken seriously by command staff, by supervisors, by you, by your partner, by your team members, by your families, suicide can be preventable. Maybe we can't eliminate suicide among cops, but we can significantly reduce the numbers. After John's suicide, SJPD changed their entire training program and told their officers that if they were depressed, they should come in; when they did they would receive counseling. Their confidentiality would be protected, and they would not be risking their badge. During the next year, twelve cops came in and received counseling. Their privacy was honored, and they have stayed on the job.

But some things have to change—in many police departments and law enforcement agencies and among cops themselves. Some of those changes are cultural.

The biggest cultural change that has to happen—among command staff, supervisors, and officers—is the belief that asking for help is a sign of weakness. Asking for help is a sign of strength, a sign of wisdom, a sign of courage. It is *not* a sign of weakness. Your reluctance to ask for help is understandable. Your whole focus is on helping others, and cops are supposed to be tough, invincible and independent. But today, we know too much about the emotional dangers of your job, and we see too many tragic situations arising from a culture that considers asking for help to be a sign of weakness, to allow ourselves to indulge in that attitude. So please: if you need help, ask for it.

I would also urge you to consider getting an annual mental health check-up, in the same way you get an annual physical or regular dental check-up. Your bosses should never mandate this, but I'm hoping they'll come to encourage you to take this step. The only way this can work is if you have access to a list of qualified mental health specialists who know about cops. Otherwise you may end up wasting your time.

San Francisco PD has developed a cadre of mental health professionals who've done ride-alongs and gone through firearms training simulator exercises as well as regular sessions with the officers in the department's behavioral science unit. Those mental health workers get what cops do and understand the stress of the work, so the officers who consult with them won't have to waste time trying to explain their work to them.

You may be still thinking to yourself, "There's no way I'm going to see a shrink if I don't have to." If that's where your head is, then I will leave you with this question, which I consider every day: If my son had had the opportunity to establish a relationship with a mental health professional before he became depressed, would he still be alive today?

As cops, you and your fellow officers also have to look out for each other. A growing number of police agencies have developed volunteer peer support programs, which pave the way for officers to serve as confidential resources for their colleagues who need help. SFPD, with a sworn force of 2,100 officers, has 300 trained peer support members. And some departments have developed a Critical Incident Response Team (CIRT). SFPD has forty officers who volunteer as CIRT members. These cops are trained volunteers with twenty-four-hour on-call responsibility (on top of their regular jobs). As CIRT members, they respond by giving emotional support when their fellow officers are involved in critical incidents.

I have the greatest respect for cops. I believe police work is the highest calling, the highest form of public service. It involves obvious risks and hidden risks. You always train for the obvious risks in your job. This father wants to tell you—and hopefully your bosses are beginning to tell you—that you have to train just as hard for the hidden risks in your job. Those hidden risks are more likely to bring you down than a bullet from a bad guy.

I wish you well in your work life and—even more important—in your personal life. God bless you all.

Appendix B

Summary of Key Books
on Police Suicide

THERE ARE A SIGNIFICANT number of excellent books on police suicide. The author at the top of any list of books on law enforcement suicide is usually John Violanti, a former New York state trooper and the leading researcher on this issue. His book, *Police Suicide: Epidemic in Blue*, is considered by many to be the most important general treatment of cops and suicide, addressing issues of the police lifestyle, stress, trauma, and suicide. Another invaluable book is *On the Edge: Recent Perspectives on Police Suicide*, co-authored by Violanti as well as Andy O'Hara, a former CHP sergeant who had his own near-suicide experience, and Teresa Tate, the survivor of a law enforcement suicide. This book, among other things, focuses strongly on police stress management. Allen Kates' book, *Cop Shock: Surviving Post-Traumatic Stress Disorder*, has been crucial in assisting both first responders and soldiers in successfully dealing with PTSD.

I am not a police officer, a psychologist, or an expert of any kind. I am the father of a police officer who took his life. In my effort to learn about cops and suicide, I have gained much from the above-mentioned works, but there are five books in this field that I have found most helpful and most valuable in helping me understand why cops die from suicide more often than they die from homicide or duty-related accidents. These same five books have also helped me come to a better understanding of what needs to be done to reduce law enforcement suicide in the future.

Thomas Joiner is the author of *Myths about Suicide*. Joiner does not focus specifically on law enforcement suicide, but his research is extremely relevant because he challenges the negative attitudes and perspectives regarding suicide. Joiner's major thesis is that suicide needs to be understood in order for us to manage and allay its fearsomeness. Joiner lost his father and maternal grandfather to suicide. "Suicide runs in my family and it is a point of honor for me to combat the thing that killed my relatives. Those who demean suicide decedents demean my dad, and in doing so, demean humanity and themselves," Joiner writes. "Survivors deserve understanding, not to mention compassion. So do those who have died by suicide; we honor them by understanding and combating their cause of death."

He points out that, in most cases, "Suicide is not an act of selfishness or cowardice. Individuals who commit suicide perceive they are a burden, they do not belong, and those closest to them will be better off if they are gone. The view of the suicidal individual is that their death will be worth more than their life to family, friends or society." They are wrong, but that is their reality. Joiner argues, "Death by suicide requires staring the product of millions of years of evolution in the face and not blinking; it is tragic, fearsome, agonizing, and awful, but it is not easy. It is not the act of a coward."

Joiner traces the historical stigma of suicide arising from the three major monotheistic religions, points out that Dante has those who committed suicide in the seventh circle of hell, and acknowledges that the resulting fear and ignorance still persists in today's society.

Joiner believes that those who die by suicide experience two thought processes at the same time: one relating to mundane daily plans and activities, the other relating to the comfort they take in the thought of ending their life. "Though it is difficult and uncomfortable to conceive of this last process, it does not change the fact that it is a true process that characterizes the minds of suicidal people. It is even more difficult to come to terms with the fact that people can harbor this very unusual state of mind at exactly at the same time they are thinking of weekend plans, or mowing the lawn, or going to the grocery store."

Police Suicide: Tactics for Prevention is a great book on the specifics of law enforcement suicide and the most effective suicide prevention approaches for police officers, especially command staff. The editors of this comprehensive work are Dell Hackett, President of the Law Enforcement Wellness Association, and John Violanti, a clinical psychologist from State University of New York at Buffalo. Hackett and Violanti are both former police officers. The other contributors are law enforcement veterans, or physicians and clinicians with extensive experience dealing with law enforcement issues. One contributor is the widow of a police officer who took his life.

Hackett points out that each year more police officers die from suicide than from homicide or duty-related accidents. He presents the key factors in serious prevention efforts: understanding the key role of trained first line supervisors; well-supported peer support and critical incident stress management programs; department leadership sending a strong and clear message to the officers that seeking help is a sign of strength, not weakness;

training all officers in appropriate listening, asking questions, and pointing out options. Hackett recommends that the training for first-line supervisors be conducted by credible, trained fellow police officers and qualified, trusted mental health professionals. The training should be presented in segments including police suicide data, those who are affected by a suicide, motivations for law enforcement suicide, dispelling common myths, and verbal and behavioral clues of suicide and major predictors of suicidal behavior. Finally, Hackett asserts, "The first barrier that must be overcome in the prevention of police suicide is the police culture itself. Police officers are reluctant to seek psychological help for fear of being perceived as weak or possibly losing their jobs."

Daniel Clark, a clinical psychologist with the Washington State Patrol, and Elizabeth White, a clinical psychologist with the Los Angeles Sheriff's Department, discuss why it is difficult for cops to seek help: the stigma of suicide and emotional problems; confidentiality concerns; job impact worries; the role of alcohol; the mistrust of the field of mental health; medication issues; and the importance of appropriate and effective intervention by friends, family, fellow officers and supervisors. They make what I think is the most important point in this entire invaluable book. In acknowledging that officers believe that asking for help is a sign of weakness, they assert that, "Supervisors and the chain of command can dispel this myth by assuring officers that seeking help is a sign of strength, not a sign of weakness."

Paul Quinnett and Vickie Watson, two other clinicians from the state of Washington, offer a brief training program so police officers can be taught to effectively intervene in the suicidal crisis of another officer. Called QPR, the intervention consists of three bold steps: questioning the meaning of possible suicide communications, persuading the person in crisis to accept help, and referring the person to the appropriate resource.

Dr. Dickson Diamond, Chief Psychiatrist for the FBI, covers departmental barriers to mental health treatment and points out that clinical depression is responsible for most suicides, including police suicides. He writes that "clinical depression is due to changes in concentrations of chemicals in the brain that regulate mood, energy, sleep, and appetite. It is not clear why some people develop this chemical imbalance, but it is clear that it has nothing to do with a weakness or a character flaw." He points out, "When depression does hit, the disease interferes with our decision-making ability and tolerance for stress." He adds: "The chemical imbalance in the brain results in such feelings of internal pain and hopelessness, so that when accompanied by impairment in judgment, decision-making and impulse control, suicide is seen as an attractive option."

Diamond believes that "Modern law enforcement has increased the risk of suicide among its own officers by discouraging the treatment of mental health disorders, such as depression, which can lead to suicide," and the implicit if not explicit message is that getting treatment for depression is a poor career move. Dr. Diamond receives more calls from supervisors who learn officers are receiving treatment than they do from supervisors where officers are showing signs of serious depression. He points out in the clearest terms that "none of the medications used to treat depression have any side effects that would impair an officer's ability to perform his or her duties," and that "these medications enhance concentration and judgment while restoring physical energy and an emotional sense of well-being." He believes that departments should be less concerned with depressed officers who are on prescribed and monitored antidepressant medication than the depressed officer who is getting no treatment at all and whose depression is limiting his or her ability to do the job and putting fellow officers at risk. Diamond acknowledges that easy access to weapons is a factor in police suicide, but his clear and firm response is, "Although easy access to a weapon is an inherent part of a career in law enforcement, easy access to mental health treatment should be as well."

In the second half of *Police Suicide,* John Violanti writes about the police culture in the context of suicide. Other chapters cover issues of trust with suicidal police officers, steps to be taken after a police suicide, and a beautiful, sad, and sensitive chapter on responding to the family survivors of police suicide by Teresa Tate, whose police officer husband took his life in 1989. She is a nationally-known advocate for law enforcement suicide survivors. She covers such specific issues as the location of the suicide, suicide in the home, notification, return of personal effects, funeral protocol, benefits, employee assistance programs, investigative reports, and the importance of how survivors are treated by police departments.

I Love a Cop by Ellen Kirschman is the best book out there for the family members and loved ones of police officers. Kirschman is a psychologist who has worked extensively with police officers and also does a lot of departmental training, especially with police departments around the San Francisco Bay area. She writes clearly about the realities of police work, the paradox between an officer's work life and his personal life, how police work changes the individual, and the physical and emotional stress as well as the organizational stress of the job. She addresses the trauma that can result from police work and also directly targets marital conflicts, domestic violence, alcohol abuse, and suicide. In addressing the issue of control, she writes, "Cops probably spend as much time controlling others as they do controlling themselves. As a matter of fact, most activities in police work have to do with controlling something or someone: traffic control, crowd control, crime control, budget control, overtime control." Cops at all levels are oriented toward control. Kirschman points to a number of the situations that can lead to suicide of police officers, including "family conflicts, relationship losses, depression, immediate access to guns, poor coping skills, financial difficulties, shame, failure, and a distorted but culturally correct sense of invincibility and independence." Kirschman adds, "More than likely their distress results from a tangled series of events and a temporarily hopeless outlook."

I recommend that every police officer in the country read *Emotional Survival for Law Enforcement* by Kevin Gilmartin. He is a former Arizona police officer turned clinical psychologist who consults with the FBI and police agencies around the country, including SFPD. He writes, "Although in many ways officers are winning the battle of street survival, they appear to be fatally losing the battle of emotional survival." He points out that cops die of suicide at a rate four times greater than being killed in the line of duty. He attacks the tendency to deny the reality of suicide or to rationalize it as simply the weakness or deficiency of the individual. He writes, "Both officers and agencies can rationalize suicide as an isolated tragedy reflective only of the events existing in the life of the deceased officer. But what about the loss and deterioration of aspects of the police officer's emotional lives, such as the destruction of functional intimate relationships, the loss of productive and loving parental roles in their children's lives, or just the loss of being happy on a daily basis? The realities of these day-to-day losses are harder to keep distance from than a suicide and can be seen without exception in any police agency." He adds, "These losses are much closer to home and much harder to deny. The suicide of police officers, although terribly tragic, is not nearly as numerically significant as the number of marriages that are lost and the number of children who grow up emotionally distant from their police parents and, unfortunately, who grow up experiencing the secondhand effects of a police career."

Gilmartin writes vividly of the danger of the "hyper-vigilance biological rollercoaster," where officers on duty are "alive, alert, energetic, involved and humorous," but when off duty, they are "tired, detached, isolated and apathetic." He points out that hyper-vigilance on the job produces a healthy amount of cynicism and mistrust, which is necessary for street survival, but off the job, can be destructive for emotional survival and relationships with family and loved ones. He repeatedly emphasizes that the very things that make cops safe and effective on the streets can harm them in their personal lives and even destroy them. Gilmartin asserts that all cop suicides, whether PTSD is involved or not, are job-related. This is a book that every cop should read.

A well-written summary of current knowledge and how-to survival steps can be found in *Bulletproof Spirit: The First Responder's Essential Resource for Protecting and Healing Mind and Heart*, by La Mesa (California) Police Captain Dan Willis. This is the best new book out there, not just for cops but for all first responders. Willis has written a readable and personally honest book with piercing stories of first responders. He also addresses the spiritual domain of first responders, providing a much-needed focus on a neglected aspect of this issue.

Bibliography

Allen, Mary. *The Rooms of Heaven*. New York: Alfred A. Knopf, 1999.

Allende, Isabel. *Paula*. New York: Harper Collins, 1994.

Barnes, Julian. *Nothing to Be Frightened Of*. New York: Alfred A. Knopf, 2008.

Bernstein, Judith. *When the Bough Breaks*. Kansas City: Andrews McMeel, 1998.

Bolton, Iris. *My Son . . . My Son*. Atlanta: Bolton Press, 1983.

Bonanno, George. *The Other Side of Sadness*. New York: Basic, 2009.

Didion, Joan. *The Year of Magical Thinking*. New York: Alfred A Knopf, 2005.

Fine, Carla. *No Time to Say Goodbye*. New York: Doubleday, 1997.

Fine, Carla, and Michael Myers. *Touched by Suicide*. New York: Gotham, 2006

Gilmartin, Kevin. *Emotional Survival for Law Enforcement*. Tucson: E-S, 2002.

Greenspan, Miriam. *Healing Through the Dark Emotions*. Boston: Shambhala, 2003.

Hines, Kevin. *Cracked, Not Broken*. Lanham: Rowman & Littlefield, 2013.

Jamison, Kay Redfield. *Night Falls Fast*. New York: Alfred A. Knopf, 1999.

Jamison, Kay Redfield. *Nothing Was the Same*. New York: Alfred A. Knopf, 2009.

Joiner, Thomas. *Myths about Suicide*. Cambridge: Harvard University Press, 2010.

Krasny, Michael. *Spiritual Envy*. Novato: New World Library, 2010.

Kirschman, Ellen. *I Love a Cop*. New York: Guilford Press, 2007.

Kushner, Harold. *When Bad Things Happen to Good People*. New York: Schocken, 1981.

Lamott, Anne. *Traveling Mercies*. New York: Pantheon, 1999.

Lewis, C.S. *A Grief Observed*. New York: Harper and Row, 1961.

Lischer, Richard. *Stations of the Heart*. New York: Alfred A. Knopf, 2013.

Martin, James. *The Jesuit Guide to Almost Everything*. New York: Harper One, 2010.

Novak, Michael. *No One Sees God*. New York: Doubleday, 2008.

Oates, Joyce Carol. *The Widow's Story*. New York: Harper Collins, 2011.

O'Connor, Flannery. *The Habit of Being*. New York: Farrar, Straus and Giroux, 1979.

O'Rourke, Meghan. *The Long Goodbye*. New York: Riverhead, 2011.

Rosenblatt, Roger. *Making Toast*. New York: Harper Collins, 2010.

Smith, Tom. *The Unique Grief of Suicide*. Wilmington: iUniverse, 2013.

Solomon, Andrew. *The Noonday Demon*. New York: Scribner, 2001.

Violanti, John, and Dell P. Hackett. *Police Suicide: Tactics for Prevention*. Springfield: Charles C. Thomas, 2003.

Wickersham, Joan. *The Suicide Index*. Orlando: Harcourt, 2008.

Willis, Dan. *Bulletproof Spirit*. Novato: New World Library, 2014.

Woefel, Joni. *Meditations for Survivors of Suicide*. Totawa: Resurrection, 2002.

Wolterstorff, Nicholas. *Lament for a Son*. Grand Rapids: William B. Eerdmans, 1987.

Young, William Paul. *The Shack*. Newbury Park: Windblown Media, 2007.